mortality,

with

friends

Made in Michigan Writers Series

GENERAL EDITORS

Michael Delp, Interlochen Center for the Arts
M. L. Liebler, Wayne State University

A complete listing of the books in this series can
be found online at wsupress.wayne.edu

mortality, with friends

essays
by
fleda brown

WAYNE STATE UNIVERSITY PRESS
DETROIT

ISBN 978-0-8143-4874-1 (paperback)
ISBN 978-0-8143-4875-8 (e-book)

Library of Congress Control Number: 2021932168

Publication of this book was made possible by a generous gift from The Meijer Foundation.

Cover design by Lindsey Cleworth

Wayne State University Press rests on Waawiyaataanong, also referred to as Detroit, the ancestral and contemporary homeland of the Three Fires Confederacy. These sovereign lands were granted by the Ojibwe, Odawa, Potawatomi, and Wyandot nations, in 1807, through the Treaty of Detroit. Wayne State University Press affirms Indigenous sovereignty and honors all tribes with a connection to Detroit. With our Native neighbors, the press works to advance educational equity and promote a better future for the earth and all people.

Wayne State University Press
Leonard N. Simons Building
4809 Woodward Avenue
Detroit, Michigan 48201-1309

Visit us online at wsupress.wayne.edu

For my friends, with love and thanks.

Contents

One wanted, she thought, dipping her brush deliberately, to be on a level with ordinary experience, to feel simply that's a chair, that's a table, and yet at the same time, It's a miracle, it's an ecstasy.

—Lily Briscoe, in Virginia Woolf's *To the Lighthouse*

Prologue

Garden

In my grandmother's fishpond were little black jelly dots with tails. I would sift them through my fingers, pass them from hand to hand like egg whites. I would turn some out onto the cement, feeling the power I had even then, inherently, to wield life or death. I was cruel, but only barely, only enough to test myself. My handprint was in the cement of the pond's edge. How valuable I was to my grandparents, how much of the world I owned already! A spring darkness was in the pool, and in the trees over it. I see it luminous, oily, and still, except for the hovering tadpoles and the goldfish. The bottom was unknown to me. I lived with so many mysteries it was as if I were swimming, keeping just above water.

What was it like, before the words took over? There was a cold pipe stuck in the tree that slowly dripped sap all summer. It was sour, dark, and thick. A drop hung on the pipe's edge for minutes before it fell. But there was no clock, only touch. During this time my parents and my grandparents lived next door to each other. To travel from one yard to the next was to engage what would become the tension that strained the elements I'm made of.

What is felt collects in the body with no comment. Where is the sun? In little islands, on the tree trunk, in the grass. There is a mimosa tree. I touch it gently and it magically folds. How full was I of all this sensation? It seems that I must have had no room for anything else. There were the red berries on the bushes under the window, the ones we told each other were poison. Who is we? My little sister, the neighbor children, the grandchildren of the neighbors. They passed through my life. I was not stupid but absorbed, forgetful. I knew the old ladies next door to my grandparents, Gertrude and Lurlene Waylan, because they had an old Victrola with a horn.

I didn't know what day it was, or what month, which goes to show that impressions make a life. I was close up. Now all I can do is approach as an interloper into what is outside of time, trying to force it into sequence. Now, and then. Light and color wash against the sky and that's all. Nothing to keep, except the word "I." I saw it. I was there.

It's adults who make up stories of their lives. What I really knew was the milkman in the driveway. He let me ride to the top of the hill sometimes on his truck. I remember mornings because I was the lone explorer. Dew was on the grass, on the hollyhocks, on the side of the milk truck. The wetness was both annoying and gratifying, evidence that I was first. Maybe my father was in the garden, as anchor, but the air had a tremulous quality, nothing certain yet.

My mind wants to rest here, for a few minutes, in relative safety, with Nana's roses budding and the gladiolas. And particularly the tightly packed petals of the peonies, with ants crawling in and out like drunkards. There is so much trouble to come, as is true, mostly, of the course of living, but here are butterflies and ants, and nicely weeded islands along the side of the house, and a garden in the back, with strawberries and marigolds and green beans. This is an argument for order. A child whose life will become often unbearable can have this forever: the garden, carefully weeded. Not standing for anything, or standing for order in the universe, or, as Elizabeth Bishop said of the carefully stacked Esso cans, evidence that somebody loves us all. Not evidence at all. Just remaining there in the mind, still wet with dew.

No matter if this child becomes a poet or a checker at Walmart, there will be this. If the child loses her way, as it is sometimes called, and entangles herself in suffering, peonies and the rest will come to her rescue not as possibilities but as wordless beauty, as helpless, as ephemeral, as a summer day.

Donna

I finish the last novel in the Neapolitan series by the writer who calls herself Elena Ferrante. Her character, also Elena, has studied her way out of the slums of Naples, grown into a writer. Her brilliant and reckless friend Lila, born, like her, in 1944, marries at sixteen and, although she never leaves Naples, barely leaves her neighborhood, becomes the passionate and furious center of intrigue and commerce. And always Elena's measuring stick: "Have I lived the life I should have?" she asks herself. "Are my caution, my dutiful studies, my relentless drive to write, excuses for not living?"

At the end, Elena has just received a package that contains the two dolls, hers and Lila's, that she thought were lost sixty years ago. Lila had thrown Elena's beloved doll down a grate into a forbidding basement. In anguish, Elena threw Lila's after. The loss had triggered events that set the series in motion: Elena's need for and rejection of, and by, her childhood friend. Now, after many years of making herself invisible, Lila, apparently, has sent the package, with no note. She had manipulated everything from the start, rescued the dolls and kept them herself. The last sentence is "I thought now that Lila has let herself be seen so plainly, I must resign myself to not seeing her anymore."

I admit I've been reading through the four weighty novels while pulling along my own echo. Maybe good stories always make us do this. My friend Donna was born six days after me, also in 1944. As I read the novels, I kept bouncing back and forth: Which was I—my friend Donna, or Elena? I am the writer. I am also the one whose early marriage was doomed from the start, who married twice more, whose life was for years in a tumult. I am also the one whose children often took second place to my studying, my drive to write, to get myself out of the neighborhood, out of my life, out of Arkansas.

My own youth was a novel I've barely heard of, not read. I was doing something else, I guess. I scroll through the many pictures I was sent of my fiftieth high school reunion. I recognize some names, some faces. Did I have friends? A fair number signed my yearbook "To Fleda, a terrific girl." But they scarcely knew me. We didn't hang out. I just seemed likeable. Someone to say hello to in the halls. I think of those years now and see myself as a ghost, somehow not attached to myself.

There was one friend. She died of cancer over twenty years ago. When I found this out, later, it felt suddenly as if the book of my youth might not have happened at all. I sometimes think if I could see her now clearly, as detailed as Lila, there would be some benefit, that my old lost self would coalesce, my edges would brighten.

Not to whine. I've been over this territory so many times before. My lost self. These years later, I can still feel the angst in my bones when I was riding the bus home from school. The dread. Of nothing in particular, only the cracking and groaning of the walls of my family's life, of mine. I can hear Robert Hayden's poem, his voice, his "fearing the chronic angers of that house." And his word "blueblack," his winter mornings, my evenings, on the bus, headed home in the dusk.

Why did Elena and Lila need each other? What did I need—an ally, a parent? I would latch on to a person, one at a time. My gaze turned only in that direction, as if we were married. There was a Sharon early on, then Donna. Donna was a fine husband, through fifth and sixth grade, and then into junior high, until Harry quickly usurped her place, with thrills she couldn't provide.

Her family owned a small house perched on one of many steep hills in Fayetteville, only a few blocks from our Leverett Elementary school. We were Mutt and Jeff, Penn and Teller: I, brown-haired, skinny, restless, giggling; she, big-boned but not heavy, fair-skinned, very blonde. Slow to laugh. Serious, forever cupping her thin hair around to cover her ears, which stood out. She was uneasy about her appearance in general. In junior high, of course, we all were. At school, she was good at everything. She worked hard. We both did. These were the early years of singling out the achievers and putting them in classes together. There was lots of competition. We were an even match at English, but she ran ahead of me in math. She had that kind of mind. We competed. We studied in her room. I see her sitting on her bed, me on the floor, books spread out. I think of her hair, soft and fine, and her ears. I am trying to bring more into focus. I can feel how it was, the algebra-anxiety, and always a sense of my rough, primal self watching my manners in her house. In anyone's house.

To be fair, my feelings were probably unremarkable. We both had the self-consciousness of our years, but her ship was more firmly anchored. Her parents would sit together after dinner with coffee and talk. Her grandmother, who lived in a nearby apartment, would be there often. An orderly life, with dessert and cups and saucers. If there was a choice, I'd usually bike up the long, steep Garland Street hill rather than have her come to my chaotic house.

At some point, her parents decided she needed a bedroom of her own, so they had one built. A change to the landscape on her behalf! Money spent! We would wander through the boards before the walls went up. Then, there it was, her room. I can't remember the colors, only the sense of newness. An amazement. In my family no one would have thought to change anything. My father rode his bike up that impossibly steep hill to teach at the university, not because he wanted to, he said, but because it was cheaper. It wouldn't wear the car out. The septic overflowed in our backyard because he didn't want to spend money to have it cleaned out. Until he had to. Nothing got fixed unless he could fix it, and then only when it had to be fixed to go on with our lives. No one would think of repainting walls, of constructing a new space. If the space had been smaller, we would have adapted.

We did adapt. When we first moved to Fayetteville, we lived in Terry Village, tiny army barracks converted for students and a few new faculty members. But then, soon, there was Donna. Donna as prototype, as harbinger. As herself. I've always felt she was counting on me. That we, like Elena and Lila, were halves of an equation. That if we got exactly balanced, some puzzle would be solved. A package might arrive in the mail, even yet, that might show me what I couldn't see, then.

I am sure those few years we had together provided essential nourishment in some mysterious way. For me, certainly. I'm not sure about her. She became a leader, a quiet, reliable member of clubs. She joined a sorority in college. She got married after graduating and moved to New York, where her parents had moved from and where they would later return. She became a medical technician. She and her husband played bridge, belonged to several charitable organizations. I don't know much, only what I read in her obituary, which I have since lost. They had at least one child.

Elena and Lila's relationship was a dance, coming together, pulling apart for years and years. Who was pulling, who pushing? Not even Elena could say. I am the writer of Donna's and my story. We had fewer years together to examine, to make a story appear at all, before—in the ninth grade—our decisive break. My next-door neighbor asked me if I'd like to go on a double date. I was fifteen. I had never been on a date. My next-door neighbor was "wild"—that was the word we used then. I was trembling with my new body, ready for anything. From that night on, I began to gradually ignore Donna, making excuses, flaunting my adventures, but always in need of the other voice, the steady one I could push against in my mind, the one that made the idea of "wild" wild. "You're always with Harry," she would say. I hurt her feelings. I know that. I was addicted, and sometimes I lied to cover my addiction. I was nonetheless inexorably bound to the needs of my flesh, which were probably not of my flesh at all, but had no other way to reveal themselves. Touch, hold on. Was I the only one of my friends who was fiercely in need, who would, who did, turn anywhere to be held? It seemed so.

I think I was using people. I think I was using Donna. I try to imagine a friendship that comes naturally, a teeter-totter equally balanced.

On early summer mornings we met while it was still cool enough and tried to teach ourselves tennis, or we walked all the way to the city pool in the scorching heat, pushing each other off the cracked sidewalks. We pulled on our shorts and walked home, still in our swimsuits. We met day after hot summer day. I try to think what we said to each other. There is in my mind a tugging that I felt between us, an unlikeness, a strain, never a fight, but a capitulation to difference, to be together. We needed to be together. I needed her, I am sure, worse than she needed me. It was imperative not to reveal that need; it was imperative not to appear to cling. My unstable being was also smart. It knew how to pretend.

The "chronic angers" of my house have been too easy an explanation. Those angers are long gone. I still feel in my bones, my blood, a deep anxiety. My own Naples, roiling with the intrigue of generations, with unresolved, unacknowledged anguish and pain. Not to mention the present added on, the guns, explosives, beheadings, called to my attention every day. I don't fault the clinging I remember. It was me, clinging to me.

Nonetheless, I did, and do, claim Donna as my friend, my best, my real friend during those years. She gave me the 45 of Elvis's "Blue Christmas" for Christmas. She lip-synched with me in my bedroom to Elvis and Ricky Nelson. The early tug of sex threw me off balance, made me reel. She went along with my lurching crazes, sometimes reluctantly.

I see her coming to my door with the gift, the record. Did I give her a gift? Was I already moving away from her at that time? That snapshot memory, and then my playing the record over and over on my player made especially for 45s. You slip the record in a slot. It was a little plastic thing, with terrible plastic sound, but I could afford it. It was mine. In my room.

I was Lila, building a kingdom in my small space. I had wrested my very own room from my family by physically moving the furniture around on one of the rare afternoons when my parents were out together, probably taking my brother to the doctor. I had asked my mother. She didn't want me to do this, but hadn't said no definitely. I took that for yes. By the time they came home, I had disassembled my baby sister's bed and moved it into my middle sister's room. I had pulled apart my own bed, moved it out of there, and assembled it again into what had been my baby sister's room. I must have been thirteen. I did that: carried the bed frames, plus mattresses, across the hall, put them together. What will! What fierce need.

Do I remember this clearly? Did I enlist my middle sister's help? She must have protested. I am sure I was a bully. The mind is its own kingdom, not to be trusted to conform to what's out there. As if what's out there is reliable, either. Do I see the same thing as my sister must have seen?

Memory re-creates itself, changing itself each time an event is recalled. We know that now. And in the case of Donna, I have so little to go on I begin to believe I invented her.

We ride our bikes to the university agri farm and climb a tall tree. She is holding on, but, I remember now, more clumsily than me. We get to the point where the branches begin to sway, where she is hanging there, afraid. "Go on, you can make it up one more branch," I taunt. So she does. She misses. I see her grab for the limb, slip, slide off the crook between two branches, and outward, to the ground, her leg landing at an unnatural angle. She grimaces, the tears well up and, quiet as she is—I remember her quietness—she begins to sob. Between her cry and my climbing on my bike to get help hangs the old familiar torment of my mind: guilt, fear, confusion. When I return with my father, the snow has started, has piled up, and she is a mound of white. We dig, but there is nothing but a pile of snow-covered leaves. I become frantic, crying, but silently, because it is a dream. My father, who has his fishing pole fastened to his bike, says we should ride a bit farther down the road and go fishing. So I grow up and she is never found.

In a novel, you either have reasons, verifiable ones, or you have some psychological truth that clarifies itself as the narrative closes down. You have a package that arrives. Yet truth doesn't close down, really. The closer you get to it, the fuzzier it seems. I ask my sister to locate Donna on the internet, but the only thing she could find was Donna's younger sister's obituary. She died young, also. Of cancer, also. "Donna's one of those people invisible on the internet," says my sister.

What was the flip side of "Blue Christmas"? I just looked it up. It's "You'll Be Gone," a song that must have disappeared as soon as it appeared. There was another song, "Oh Donna," sung by Richie Valens. The refrain went, " 'Cause I love my girl, Donna, where can you be?"

On our first real date, my husband Jerry sang that one to me in the car. I tell him I married him because he made me feel like home.

I was being urged to come to my fortieth high school reunion. I was by then living in Delaware and had been for a while, an academic, a writer, detached from my flesh-and-bones past. What friends did I have that I'd want to see again? Donna. I wrote back, "I'll come if Donna does." The message came back, "I'm so sorry to tell you. . . ."

Someone told me Donna's brother was living in Fayetteville, in their old house. He gave me the address of Donna's son. So I wrote him and he wrote back, a long letter. He said the last thing his mother told him was that he needed to be strong. I said I wrote poetry. He said he wrote song lyrics, and he sent me a lot of them. He seemed glad to hear from someone who had known his mother well. He said he hadn't. And I seemed to bring her presence to him a little. I could sense his drifting, his immaturity. I had the urge to step in, to be his mother, to grab hold of him and point him in some clear direction. Donna inhabited me, told me she was worried about him.

We imagine ourselves in our lives at a pinnacle of awareness, and we are. This is our time; we're alive only now. I feel responsible for gathering the facts so that not so much is lost. I write to hold on to not just the facts, but the feel of my time, the tone. I look for connections. We are all related. Isn't there a thrill when we discover a long-lost person related to us in some way? One more link in the chain of our inheritance, in who we "are." Ancestry.com thrives on it. There was a short piece in the newspaper in Arkansas years ago, something about the DAR, I think. A woman was reported to have said, "I've traced my ancestry all the way back to Adam."

I knew myself as not-Donna. I swung outward, she held on. She stood there, in the deep center of my mind, quizzical, amused at my silliness, alarmed at my risks. I survived, have survived through marriages, divorces, my own cancer. She died at forty-nine. When I think about this long enough, I have a strong feeling of unreality, which makes me swing in the other direction, to bring her here again, to verify our existence.

Smoke

I will describe it since most of you weren't there. The fifties and sixties, when I was growing up, looked like London during the coal-burning days. Heavy haze. Ashtrays placed like art objects on coffee tables. Ceramic or glass, gracefully curved, with their thumb-print indentations for the cigarette. Beautiful women tilting their fiery emphasis in magazine ads. Katharine Hepburn, Cary Grant, Barbara Stanwick, Bogey and Bacall speaking their lines through the tantalizing filter of smoke.

Smoke, bless its heart, could be called into service as your personal angel, the messenger between you and the unseen, while you were describing how to baste a turkey, or the finer points of archery, or your mother's meddling. Transcendence rose nonchalantly from the mundane. It filled the space between you and another as if neutrinos were visible, so that what happened on all levels became linked in a noncommittal way, became warmed by holding it inside long enough to absorb the poisons we all could share. Yes, this will kill me, this is my silent declaration that I know I will die and am willing—not just willing but standing here participating in the process of both enjoyment and dissolution, making an artistic response, a kiss and a silent whistle and a dismissal, a dismissal in the kindest way, upward, to mingle with the angels.

At the University of Arkansas, star-shaped ashtrays pressed from heavy foil were provided on the corner of every desk. If everyone smoked, style, then, was a delineation. Bethany Dumas, my graduate student creative writing instructor, pulled a fiercely strong unfiltered English Oval from its box with a panache I immediately scoured the local stores to emulate. Dr. Kimpel smoked as if he could hardly be bothered, hand quickly to the mouth as punctuation, blowing the smoke out delicately for such a big man. He knew everything in the world; smoke was the engine that carried it. Get this done, this smoking thing. Dr. Eaves smoked as if it were part of the art of living, the hand raised to the mouth, two fingers pressed tenderly against the lips, the inhale, the exhale, oh glorious, the release. Glorious wry smile, slow trickle of smoke. There he is, quoting Byron assailing Keats: "Here are Johnny Keats' piss-a-bed poetry. . . . No more Keats, I entreat: flay him alive; if some of you don't I must skin him myself: there is no bearing the driveling idiotism of the Mankin."

Exhale, chuckle.

In the scruffy bathroom on the first floor of Old Main—back when it was Old Main and not renovated, basically, as a museum—two sofas stared across from each other. Between classes, smoke billowed out the door each time it swung open. We loved each other, we loved our comradeship of smoke, our Zippo flip-lid lighters with Razorback Hogs etched on them, or engraved initials, or sleek gold trim. We loved our cigarette packs, plain, boxed, or with fancy cloth covers that snapped closed, we loved the ritual zipping of the strip to remove the plastic on the top, the pulling back of the seal to open the gold foil lining, the tapping of the pack against a table to allow one cigarette to slide forward, the packing down of the single cigarette against a chair arm, or desk, as if the density of the tobacco were of great concern. We loved the first drag, we loved the word "drag," carrying its darkness behind it like a cloak, its cloaked rebellion, its rebellion against healthy living, against childhood. Those who didn't smoke weren't exactly ostracized but stood outside the magic circle. It was truly a magic circle, a sacred space where no words mattered, only the telling smoke between words, through words, carrying words on its back.

When I was ten or eleven, I walked to Bachmann's General Store at the lake and bought a pack of candy cigarettes. Practicing. My first real one was on a Girl Scout camping trip. Older, cooler Judy gave me one. But then, to my eyes, everyone was cooler. Indeed, most of my friends could sing along with a slew of popular songs, but not me. Not many. Most of my friends wore matching sweater sets and Bobbie Brooks clothes. Not me. None of my friends had a severely brain-damaged brother at home, one who had seizures. And a father who yelled about money. At least not that I knew of. I didn't know much, though. What I did know was that adults smoked. My parents didn't smoke and didn't drink, not because they had any religious qualms, but because, it seemed, they were as out of the mainstream as I was. All the world was drinking, smoking, dancing, and watching TV. Finally, finally, we had a little portable TV, but the rest I had to begin inventing for myself.

My first real cigarette: I lay at the edge of the tent, facing outward—acetone, acetic acid, ammonia, arsenic, benzene, butane, carbon monoxide, lead, formaldehyde—all 4,800 chemicals, alerting me to their surprised circulation throughout my tender young body, my cheek scratching against the dirt to draw in as much fresh air as possible.

Stomach lurching, head spinning. I have had that feeling since—and this is another large private room of my past—during chemo and radiation, the same initial scream of horror the body makes when it realizes it's being poisoned.

I do not remember how long after my first cigarette that I rode my Schwinn to the little store about a mile away and sheepishly purchased a pack of Salems for 29 cents. My guess was, menthol would work like an antidote to the discomfort. After all, didn't you rub it on your chest when you had a cold?

I am in awe, still, at how we invite suffering as a way to alleviate suffering. All the time. How we yell at people we love in order to get more love; how a girl has sex with an abusive boy, to feel wanted; how Donald Trump fought to the top of the mountain, where all the trouble is, to muffle the dark cries in his heart. How the ache of my own young heart was soothed by lying in the field behind my house, often with my much "wilder" neighbor, flicking away grasshoppers and blowing smoke over the tops of the weeds. No one could see us. We'd cleared our own place in the world at last, rocking the boat, disrupting expectations.

I suspect this is how my mother felt years before, when she lit a Lucky Strike with her neighbor in Middlebury. We'd moved there for the year for my father to teach, alien territory especially for my mother, a timid Midwesterner. At last she made a friend. At last her own choice. The friend smoked, so she did, too, until my father's disdain was too much to bear.

Harry was eighteen and in college, I was fifteen, when I first climbed into the back seat of a friend's car to go on a "date." Harry smoked Tareytons. Lots of them. So I did, too. I told you, those years were shrouded in smoke, hiding my life from myself. We married when I was seventeen, because my family had moved away from our old town, I would say, but I suppose it was my fierce need for love, for being held, for growing up. Reflection does not necessarily clarify. True, too, I longed to be back home. So, how gloriously alive and separate, to be traveling together back to my hometown in our newly purchased Chevy, back south, neatly folded new clothes in my suitcase, touching a cigarette to the dashboard's glowing bull's-eye lighter, tapping ash into the little pull-out ashtray!

In one of my other lives, the ones I've been able, after this time, to see running parallel, my grandfather pays my tuition to Yale, his alma mater. I study with famous poets, I work out the sturm and drang of my life wildly, recklessly, straight-on courageously. I live through it. I become and become. Instead, in this other life, I finish high school, enroll at the University of Arkansas, graduate from there, take all my degrees, as a matter of fact, from there, because there is where I was, with my two children, after the gut-wrenching divorce. I climb, grip by uncertain grip, up the cliff of my life into the light.

Harry and I married in 1962. The surgeon general's report on the scientifically proven dangers of smoking, its link to lung cancer, came out in 1964. Gradually, the cigarette became the symbol of our difference. I would quit. I would urge him to quit. He would say he had quit except for the pipe. He would say he wasn't inhaling, but he was. He would surreptitiously smoke cigarettes all day at work. The cigarette stood for my disappointment in him as a person. He knew that. He could feel me yearning outward. The sadness and anger built. He drank more.

Once, when he was inarticulately enraged at me, he forced a cigarette in my mouth. I had quit. He said I was sanctimonious. No, that's not a word he would have used. Words were my weapon, not his. He forced my mouth open, shoved in the cigarette, and lit it. "You think you're so high and mighty," he might have said. That would be language he could use. He wanted me to come back to him, in my mind. I know that. He wanted me to be the seventeen-year-old he remembered. She was never who he remembered, but she was, inside, silent as to who she was. She was working it out. She needed someone to be with while she worked it out. She was not guiltless, nor was she guilty. She didn't know what she was doing. She wanted something that smoking a cigarette seemed to stand for. She had drifted like smoke into this life, and gradually she had come to spy another life across the way, far off and undefined, but shining in clear air.

Years later, Kelly, our daughter, stood by her father's hospital bed while the doctor said, "Harry, if you don't quit smoking and drinking, you're going to die. Soon." She heard that. She was studying to be a therapist. She tried to rally his family. "Oh, Kelly, you're making too much of this. You're stirring up trouble. Leave it alone," they all said. Her first lesson in denial. And another lesson in helplessness. When he died at fifty-five, he was still smoking.

I was still smoking when Harry and I divorced. But I was going to quit, I was sure. I promised myself I would only smoke in the evenings. After one three-hour evening seminar, I looked at my butt-filled ashtray and realized I was on my way to smoking an entire pack before bedtime. That was it, the end of cigarettes for me. On the first of two dates I had with Dennis, before we precipitously decided to marry, he told me he was thinking of quitting smoking. I told him it would be hard for me if he smoked. So he quit, cold turkey. As he had quit drinking, years ago, cold turkey.

The word "quit" comes, in its oldest sense, from Latin *quietus*, a past participle of *quiescere* 'be still,' from *quies* 'quiet.' Cravings can be quieted, but they sneak undercover down other alleys.

Alcoholics know this, that stopping drinking doesn't stop the internal craving that may turn into gambling, sex addiction, overeating, for example. Dennis, well, it seemed that I had walked unsuspecting into an explosion of symptoms. Smoking was not one of them.

When that marriage was over, I started going out with Jerry, a longtime smoker. No surprise, since he's four years older than I am, and grew up in that same communal haze of smoke. The relief of finally seeing possibilities for joy was enough to start me smoking again. My first cigarette after many years was with my friend Kathy, as we drank beer in the afternoon and told each other how miserable we were. Good old cigarettes. Nothing better for that purpose, to hold and wave in the air, to illustrate, to suck smoke in like a declaration of defiance, to blow out it like a sigh. Our mutual sign language.

I knew, I was adamant, that it couldn't go on—the smoking. I told Jerry he just couldn't smoke. He said he'd quit. I'd heard that before. His former wife had also been at him about this.

I quit. He quit. He will not like me to tell the rest of this. Months later I reached into the pocket of his coat hanging in the closet. I don't know why I did. I had a nagging feeling. There was a packet of cigarettes. It was as if he'd slept with another woman. Well, it felt like that: a betrayal of trust. He'd lied to me. Jerry, the most honest human I knew, lied to me. At first he tried to lie his way out of it. His fear of my wrath, my disappointment, my turning away from him, was greater than his need for honesty. Which just shows the intense power of cigarette addiction, more so than heroin.

He did quit at last. Nothing clarifies the intensity of addiction like trying to quit. The mind, the whole body, is pulled as if by gravity, toward the next cigarette. I hated it. I felt trapped, not the captain of my own fate. I've scrounged wastebaskets for stubs, I've smoked them down into the filter, I've walked miles to the store. And I don't even consider myself a heavy addict. I was able to cut down to two a day, a number of times. Smoking always seemed alien to my body, not something that was naturally "in" me to do but driven by circumstance and psychology.

But, basically, isn't it indigenous, beloved? Cannabis wafted from hookahs in 5000 BC, and from shamanistic rituals in 4000 BC. Greeks took vapor baths in hemp seed. When Europeans arrived in the Americas in the fifteenth century, they spread their pipe-smoking habit. Opium smoking reached its pinnacle in the nineteenth century. During World War I, cigarettes were tucked into mess kits for soldiers, little gifts from the government. Evil or medicinal, dangerous or sociable, we have loved our smoke. I loved my smoke.

"He sighed one last lung-deep plume toward the ceiling and put out his king-sized cigarette in an ashtray on the glass table at his side of the king-sized bed." How could Updike tell us this without the cigarette? Oh, yes, I'd forgotten, they came in king size, regulars, charcoal filters, and the unfiltered Lucky Strikes that left chunks of tobacco on your tongue and made you feel like a tough woman, or a cowboy. The little prop for any number of private movies, or scenes in novels.

It has been over forty years since I quit, if you forget that one lapse.

My mother's parents held strong sway over me, at least in my mind, since my parents hardly seemed to know what to do with their lives. Nana did, and it was to live decorously, to pay attention to what people thought of you, to pinch your cheeks to make them less wan, to use something called "Baby Touch" (basically sandpaper) on your legs when you were old enough for them to sprout obvious hair. Certainly to abstain from smoking, because ladies didn't smoke. Granddaddy had his pipe stand, pipes, and thermidor, but that was relegated to his corner, a proper man's space. What these images have to do with anything is that they formed a mirror of my life. The wish to fit in, to do things decorously, as well as the lurking suspicion that I was not that, not decorous, not "normal." My family wasn't normal, my father, compared to other fathers, seemed aboriginal (it was years later before the word "Asperger's" was commonplace). My brother lived in a maelstrom of seizures, drool, bloodied nose, and inarticulate sounds. Not normal.

I was aiming my sextant, trying to find the North Star. Was "normal" to the north? Then what was this undertow that edged me off course? What was it that made me choose Elvis over Ricky Nelson, bad boy over good? What was it that drove me into the back seat of that car at fifteen doing what fifteen-year-olds supposedly weren't doing, at least not ones like me, professor's kids, churchgoing kids? Heading to a car to smoke during lunchtime, like the vocational ed students.

After I married Harry, Nana said when they visited, "Your teeth used to be so white." That's all. What was unseen wafted between us thick as smoke. I couldn't wait to step out on our little balcony and light up.

My teeth are white now. Goodbye to the cigarette, to the Marlboro Man, to that particular way to invite suffering. Goodbye to James Baldwin, his anger released in thin vapors that suggested how much more there was of it. Goodbye to the fantasy of Doris Day, her cigarette as seemingly harmless as cotton candy. Goodbye to those of us who remember having less to fear, who imagined there was less to fear, who are only just now waking up, as if the Surgeon General had surprised us this morning, standing at our door like a Jehovah's Witness, saying, "Listen, can you see? Cigarettes are not the issue. You're here. The sky is clear, so now you have to deal with that."

The Moment

No sound from the kids, not for fifteen minutes. I trust they're asleep. I get my tiger-striped chenille robe off the back of the bathroom door and put it on over my jeans and flannel shirt. I am that cold. Lately I stand sometimes for an entire half-hour over the floor furnace. Other times I read curled up along the wall with my feet out over the heat that drifts upward of its own accord, no blower to send it around the house. There are advantages to this kind of heat. There's always a place to go, to get to it, a center in the house.

It's an old house that my husband agreed, in desperation, to buy two years before, borrowing money from his mother to do it. I had been depressed, aimless, and vacant: a mother-machine, with a new baby, and Kelly, who would soon be five. Maybe I shouldn't have stayed at home with the kids. I wanted to. I wanted to feed them carrot sticks and read them Dr. Seuss. But the truth is, having a job would have only delayed the inevitable.

I would go to the drug store and stare at the bright bottles of hair-spray, plastic travel kits, and see them, not as things to buy but as permanent art objects, attached to the walls. I would stand in the aisle, confused about where the exit was. I would pick Kelly up, trying to push Scott's stroller and carry him at the same time, as if I were a beast of burden, dumb and thoughtless. I would start longing for something I couldn't afford, like the brass colonial lamp I saw in the window of Miller's. My life would be at a standstill, without the lamp. I would sell my body to get it. I scarcely remembered having a body.

On this evening I watch my husband walk into the living room and sit down on the sofa, his skinny legs barely touching his khaki pants. He is rigid with fear, as he's been for almost a year, waiting for this to happen. I've taken a Valium in preparation. I took it an hour ago, so it would be working by now. Normally, I'm not a drug user of any kind if I can help it, not even aspirin, but there will never be another moment like this one. I take a breath.

✳   ✳   ✳

The couple opening the door to Ed McMahon with the huge check—it's usually only a couple of years before the money's gone. No matter what, people tend to shift with circumstances, but come back to the set point of who they are. There's no great pivot of before and after. The before has been climbing uphill for a long time, our breathlessness, like Keats upon a peak in Darien, only stored-up anticipation. Where are we but where we knew we would be?

What I have to say to him is a turmoil of particles of the past, squeezed into a few words. The moment, like all moments, empty and full, on the verge and passing. This one firing deep in the limbic system, the hippocampus, driving waves of amnesia throughout the body. What was it like? I can't say anymore, and I couldn't have said then, but I will call it holy, that precise moment, because it is set apart in my mind, elevated like an offering to the gods—a moment when the heart is reamed out deeper than one imagined, and all these years later deserves its own kind of honor, for the sake of the simple, unresolved human life we all share.

Octoraro Creek

T he bank was too steep to climb down—almost a cliff, dense with leaves—to the roaring Octoraro Creek. On the hillside, the roots of small trees gripped the soil like old women's hands, deceptively delicate-looking. The house itself was barely a house, more a red A-frame hunting shack, perched on the edge. There's something about vertigo, about appearing to barely hold back slippage, that attracted me, attracts me, the way it must have attracted Frank Lloyd Wright at Falling Water. The tension of an uncertain fulcrum. The way a poem unseats me: the fear and joy of not having a handhold.

Inside it was a bit like the cabin of a boat: a bench for a sofa, a small table and two chairs, miniature kitchen, miniature bathroom. Did it have a shower? I think so. You climbed stairs almost as vertical as a ladder to get to the loft, where a mattress lay on the floor. From up there, looking out a window, you could seem to hover.

It was desperation. It was a desperate longing to plant myself there, away from the university, away from town, from I-95. If I couldn't live in my beloved cottage on our lake in Michigan, I'd have a Delaware version, or, rather, over the state line into Maryland. Rising Sun, Maryland. How can you not want to live in a place called Rising Sun?

Away from my ex-husband. I didn't say that to myself. I don't like to talk about it because that marriage was so insane I would like to think it wasn't me living it, but some intoxication I recovered from. Which is basically the truth. The illness of my life, my unconsciousness. My daily nursing him from his own terrors, his suicidal tendencies, his swings from sweet and thoughtful to fiercely, blindly angry. But who wants to hear all that? All bad marriages are the same. No matter how they're described, the describer always subtly comes out up there in the loft, looking down at the river: the sane one, the one who Sees Everything Now. Enough to say that I myself emerged, after years of therapy, blinking like a mole in daylight, unsteady on my feet.

He bought our house from me, so I had half a house's worth of money sitting in the bank. I knew what I wanted. To look at water, to nestle, yes, nest in the trees. This was years before I could see my way to owning the Michigan cottage. Years before I retired, before the thought of actually living in Michigan entered my head. This would be my place, looking down on the Octoraro Creek as it poured over rocks, bubbled over branches, roared around the bend. And down the road, there was a tiny pond and beach. I could get a little rowboat. I could lie on the beach in the sun. I could see that exactly.

That pond. Almost as soon as I signed the papers, I began worrying that it would go away. Fill up with silt. No one would want to dredge it. And who would replenish the beach sand? Would we be the only ones who cared? It wasn't really a neighborhood—just a rough collection of houses, some the kind with cars on blocks beside the house. Certainty feeds on resistance. The perfection of a dream is in direct proportion to the danger of its collapse.

It seems that after a divorce many people have a period of temporary insanity. I had a friend back in Arkansas, a mother of two, who, after her breakup from her minister husband, turned into a full-fledged hippie, with the long paisley dress, beads. After my first marriage ended, I took up for a while with an ex-Marine who'd been a sniper in Vietnam. His favorite occupation was target shooting with his .44. This time, after my second divorce, a friend of mine who owned a house on Octoraro Creek told me there was a tiny place just down the road from her for sale. I drove out to look. I had to have it: I felt as if I were cracking through my paved-over life to let water spring from it again. No, that wasn't it. I had been shut down. I had been dead. I was reviving.

Reasons come after the fact. The deep movements occur, the deep rivers of the self surface in emblems. River. House. Deck. Trees. They spread themselves out in a panorama that stands for us, for me. I knew that even then, but desire doesn't change its mind just because it sees through itself. This would be my Michigan. This would be my return.

I should mention that by this time I was dating Jerry. Dating: such a funny word for when middle-aged people begin to spend time together. Then more time. We were at a cusp, by this time, of commitment. I was unwilling to make it, so the Octoraro Creek project was ostensibly all mine. So I pretended. No, I really did imagine I was still able to walk away from the relationship. I was still unsure of it. I was a "ghostly galleon tossed upon cloudy seas." That's from "The Highwayman," by Alfred Noyes. I was that old poem's turmoil and passion, minus its certainty. Bess, the landlord's daughter, loved the highwayman enough to shoot herself to warn him of the British lying in ambush for him. But when Jerry and I spent our first night in my newly purchased minipa-radise, waking under the eaves, tangled in sheets, I had a shudder of fear. I did not want us. I wanted myself. There. I felt that I could live alone forever. I didn't say this. Yet later, we sat on the tiny deck with our coffee, and then we took the long way around to get to the creek bed. He took my hand, rock to rock. I had this feeling of being cared for, looked after. Seen. A new thing. So there I was, convincing myself first one way, then the other.

The previous owner showed me the plans he'd had made for a house he was thinking of building on the site. Jerry went with me to an architect, and we commissioned him to design a house, all wood and glass, leaning out as far as possible over the creek. My house. Well, by this time we thought we'd both live in it. Until now my life had been driven by all sorts of ghostly emotional tossings that I was apparently helpless against. Never had I been able to live in a house that felt like me. Never had I been able to live just where I wanted. The Octoraro Creek was a long way from the university where I taught, where Jerry and I both taught, but that seemed a welcome escape.

The drive out there was exquisite, forty minutes through rolling hills, horse farms, little traffic. A small tavern and a café were the only amenities along the way. You turned off the main road and wound along a narrow road through hills and valleys, and finally the hairpin road to the property. Except for my artist friend, the other neighbors appeared to be laborers, truckers, people who liked their lives as unencumbered by civilization as was possible in that part of the country.

When the plans were complete, still professing to be single, I took Jerry with me to consult a builder. My friend Jerry, with whom I was going to build a house. A house that was going to cost too much. Still, it made perfect sense to me.

I planned a surprise fiftieth-birthday party for Jerry at my apartment. My first party there. Jerry was surprisingly subdued. After everyone had gone home, we sat on the floor among the silly gifts. A moment of silence. Quietly, as is his way, he told me that the builder had discovered we couldn't get a permit to build on the land. It wouldn't perk for more than the tiny bathroom there now. What I remember is a sense of desperation beyond reasonable. Terror, almost.

People don't talk much about the joy of terror, although moviemakers have made money on it, poets and novelists have lingered in its icy grip. No, terror's too strong. Terror is what you feel when you're about to be shot, or fall to your death. The joy, the pleasure, is in freefloating, the loss of a point of view you can trust. You're desperate for a hold, but at the same time, you know you will never be more alive.

Thus began the saga. There was a tense meeting with the realtor, who said he had no idea. We contacted the former owner, who said he had no idea. He had even drawn up plans of his own for an eventual house on the property. This was rural Maryland, and apparently the deed had passed from hand to hand without anyone looking back in the records to see. I had spent all that money on land that wouldn't perk. What now? A contained septic system that would need to be drained? Not feasible, I was told. I have to say, for a person who had had a ton of therapy at this point, I was desperately flailing. Jerry flailed along with me, bringing his managerial skills to this problem, which was now ours. Showing me how it was, with him. Total commitment. Okay, I thought, I'll sell that property and buy the property next door. They wouldn't sell. Okay, I'll buy the piece down the road a bit. Not as close to the water, but Jerry and I paced it off and saw that it would be okay. No, the cost of building would be too high. At one point I even visited a mobile home lot to see what it would cost to move one up there. But they said the road was too twisting, couldn't do it.

I decided to go to the bank and plead my case. I should have been informed about the restriction. The bank had supposedly inspected. They should have caught it. Yes, they should have. I met, trembling, with the bank manager, who said, of course, there was nothing that could be done.

When we look back, we tend to imagine our past as some sort of necessary path to get us where we are now, which we interpret as a location. A place. But I think the underground river is always doing its work, not taking us to some "conclusion" which is "now," but simply expressing itself in a multitude of ways. The Octoraro Creek is 22 miles long, a tributary of the Susquehanna River that winds into the Chesapeake Bay. It crosses the Mason-Dixon line. It has an east and a west branch and drains 208 miles of watershed. All of this is creek, all different, all the same. It changes expression. The meaning of the creek is not the bay. Its purpose is not to fill the bay, but to be water, on the move. What this says about me I'm not sure, except that these years later, living in Michigan on Grand Traverse Bay and only a few miles from our cottage, I see that earlier time as a legitimate expression, what I was able to do within the constraints of the life I had then. My panic? A fear that, after all, I would not get to be who I am, would not be allowed to marry water and trees forever.

Likewise, my previous marriage was a legitimate expression. I beat myself up for making such a poor choice. Choice? Was I the maker of myself? Could I form myself into someone with good sense? He was my dream. Star graduate student, handsome, charming, funny, good cook. That's what I saw. The best of all possible men. At least of those available. I married him so quickly, oh, there is where I really begin to cringe. The children. What happens when a parent is unconscious, lets herself be carried away by her own romantic imaginings? She lets herself and her children in for years of trouble. The rocky shoals, the sharp twists. Interesting enough to look at from far above.

Finally, there was nothing to do but put the Octoraro Creek property up for sale, making clear its restriction, and look for something else. Of course nothing else measured up. Everything was too civilized. What I really wanted, of course, was the cottage in Michigan. Or my old, almost corporeal imagining of it. Unfinished walls, old fireplace, the musty smell of winter. What we finally found was another small house, built as a vacation home, in a community with a shared beach on the upper Elk River that also opened into the Chesapeake Bay. Now I owned two houses.

And now it's time to admit my renovation mania, ongoing and as deep as my previous mania for the right house. I have asked myself, what is it I want? What is the vision that will press me somehow more tightly to the earth? What beauteous exoskeleton will provide that vision? What vase, what shelf, what grand sofa, will balance me on the side of the hill with the perfect degree of tension? What words, what songs, what poems?

We had parquet squares installed in the entire downstairs. The waxed ones had so much richer gleam than the ones with polyurethane finish. No matter that I was down on my hands and knees polishing just to keep them respectable. We took the kitchen cabinets apart, spread them out on the living room floor, sanded and painted them. We tiled the countertop. We replaced the metal stair rails with wood. I lay awake all night one night because Jerry wanted to stain and varnish them. I wanted to paint them white. How could I live with stain? Something in my deep soul is wracked in the presence of what feels like a poor aesthetic choice. But I lived with it and I lived with Jerry and, in good time, reader, I married him. When we revisited the attorney in Elkton, Maryland, to change the deed to reflect our marriage, she seemed overjoyed that we had quit living in sin.

So we transformed our house. We added a lower deck, put up a hammock, raked away gravel at the end of the long driveway, planted hundreds of periwinkle sprouts. We planted evergreen trees everywhere they might grow. We spread wood chips to make a path to the back path to the water. We bought a big canoe, and rollers to get it to the Elk River. We took it out and fought the waves. The river at that point was a stretch wide enough for tankers to make their way from the Delaware Canal to the open Chesapeake Bay. When they came by, they could almost swamp us. Swimming, too, required hard work against a strong current. But we had this: a seclusion of woods, a house that, when the leaves were off the trees, you could see a glint of water from the deck.

That was before the property behind and to the left of us was bought by a man who ran his bush hog down "our" path (which turned out to be his) so his boys could have better access with their ATVs. That was before our next-door neighbor decided to cut all the trees in his front yard to put in a swimming pool that never materialized. I curled up on our balcony, my sobs not at all drowning out the saws.

All of which goes to show you can't keep a perfect tension forever, or even for long. I've spent almost thirty years sitting on a cushion every day, staring at a wall, learning that, and still, my skin remains as sensitive as a sunburn. The difference meditation makes is that the sunburn is only that, rather interesting to watch, even if it hurts. And the vision of Octoraro Creek is only that, a vision. What I made of it in my mind.

Like people. Like my terror of marrying Jerry. How can you really see someone? And if I could see him, what would I see? A river, sweeping around the rocks, softening in the deep spots, smoothing, with that underneath motion that pulls along a leaf even when all looks still. He shifts. People are not stationary objects. But even in that shifting, which is really a shifting in my mind, he has the nature of his own self: calm, gentle, tender. I cut his hair; I trim his beard. That's as far as I go toward renovation.

After we had lived in the house near the Elk River for nearly a year, we got a call from our realtor friend, Fred. "Is there any reason in hell you wouldn't take $16,000 for the Octoraro Creek property?" he asked. A huge loss, but no, no reason in hell.

Mildred

When she comes to the water, we don't see her. We don't see her when she goes in. We hear the splashing, we see the paw prints, the five long claws. She lives under the cottage, in our life's shadow. We see where she enters. With our allusive and complicated brains, we decide to make her stand for what was there before we were. She is probably not the same raccoon. They live only one to three years. We give her an imagined continuity. We name her Mildred after Mildred Osborne, the now-deceased next-door neighbor, for no reason other than to keep the Osbornes around a while longer, although the new people, new for the last ten years, are better neighbors—that is, they take the kids out on their jet skis and motorboat, neither of which we own.

Mildred decides to have babies upstairs in our cottage crawl space. John, the carpenter remodeling our kitchen, says he hears scuttling and scuffling above his head. Our other neighbor, Lou, says we should set a trap to catch Mildred and drown her. There are too many "Mildreds" getting into trash buckets, he says. John says we should get poison or something. Or shoot her. I think maybe my sensitivity is too precious for their older world. I think of my father and his brother, out with their shotguns killing crows, squirrels, anything that came along, as if the world would last forever.

I call the SPCA. The young woman tells me they can't come get a raccoon. She tells me to soak a rag in ammonia and to play loud music near the crawl space to drive her out.

I forgot to say Mildred got into the cottage by crawling down the chimney. And then up the stairs. I think I will drive her out, then crawl in and get her babies, put them in a box, and take them to a place where she can move them elsewhere. I soak the rag and set it just inside the crawl space. I can see nothing in there, in the dark. I get my little red radio and tune in the loudest music, which turns out to be Christian rock. All night in my sleep or semisleep, the Christians are letting me know they are here, and up to date.

The morning mist is rising and there is Mildred pacing the roof of the cottage. She sees me. I imagine she sees me, although raccoons have very poor distance vision. Maybe she senses me. We look in each other's direction for a long minute, two mothers. We know each other. We know nothing of each other. I continue with my plan. I block the opening to the fireplace. I get a cardboard box. I go upstairs and open the crawl space. It is dark in there. There is loud scuffling and hissing and miniature growling beyond the range of my flashlight. I don't know how old the babies are. They may be almost ready to leave the nest. They may have grown very sharp claws and teeth. I back out of the crawl space. I take the ammonia-soaked rag with me. I have already turned off the music, which was still blasting in Jesus's name.

I go downstairs and remove the piece of steel that we use to close up the fireplace in winter. I set aside the bucket I used to hold it tight against the fireplace opening. I go back out in the woods and watch the roof, where Mildred is still pacing. I tell her without speaking that I give up. She lumbers to the chimney and slowly lowers herself. I do not know how she knows, except for maybe the draft of air rising now. When she is all the way in the chimney, she stops and looks at me again before she lowers herself out of sight.

I Take Thee

I was out for a walk. In the Historic Barns Park near where we live, near the restored barns and botanical garden, there is a sunken area that used to be the basement of a large building, its beautiful stone foundation walls still intact. A new wood fence has been built around the upper rim to make the space itself private, even if outdoors. You can walk by and peer over the edge, although if you lean in too close, you could be seen. Today, I'm surprised to see there's a wedding down there, all white wrought-iron arch and lilies! I'm in shorts myself, standing back, just over the heads of the couple under the arch. The audience sits quietly in folding chairs, flowers all around, as if they were buried. It is mid-ceremony. I am barely breathing. I've intruded upon this moment, this ceremonial sealing of vows, the energy of the universe intentionally poured into this cup of space.

The feeling is beyond words. Kevin Shilbrack, in his collection of essays, *Thinking Through Rituals*, writes, "One of the greatest obstacles to a philosophy of ritual, in my judgment, has been the view that language must be about empirical facts if it is to be even possibly true. Given this view, ritual language (and religious language generally) is in a difficult situation if it is not to be taken as meaningless babble." He considers: after Wittgenstein rejected the idea that language has to describe to be useful, John Austin argued that we can actually accomplish things with words. We can christen a ship, pronounce a couple married. Language can enact real changes in the world. Prayer and sacrifice, for example, are more than just "symbolic." They rearrange our feelings; they shift the universe.

Sometimes. Maybe this time. Maybe not. There's a video of a bride singing Christina Aguilera's "The Right Man" at her own wedding. A blogger writes, "To me, this serenade was not an act of love, but an act of vanity. I saw a woman in the midst of a performance that had nothing to do with how she felt about the man she was walking towards and everything to do with a fantasy she'd been playing out in her head since she was a little girl, groom to-be-determined."

The blogger may be right, but she'd do well to express a little empathy. No matter what, a wedding is a woman's (mostly hers, I'd say) big chance to step into elegance. She gets to be the star. My sister and I put pillowcases on our heads and promenaded around the bedroom, singing, "Here comes the bride, big fat and wide!" Funny, because the bride, of course, is supposed to be beautiful, more perfect and perfectly adorned than she's ever been. You might think virgin, a few generations back. Think how "virgin" implies "without sin." As in extra-virgin olive oil. Fresh, not cooked.

And there's the cultural pressure, the ages-old narrative drive toward the fantasy ending, the comic ending in the Shakespearean sense. Lysander and Hermia, Demetrius and Helena, and Theseus and Hippolyta—everyone gets matched up. There's a beginning (girl meets boy, or any variation of that) and an end (girl marries boy, ditto). After which comes the following narrative, with its wider variation and looser structure, the one that ends in death or divorce. The hereafter of that other story, with its own ritual punctuation. Somebody speaks words.

Philosophers deal in words. But I wonder if words can carry the load. I'm pretty sure that even if, even if, all the bride meant was to have everyone see her in the most beautiful dress she'll ever wear, she can't help but feel lightning strike. I'm sure for a second, at least, she stands utterly vulnerable, wordless, in the way that joy momentarily strips us of the trappings we thought we needed.

I'm tearing up, myself, watching the exchange of rings. The greater the joy, the more fraught with loss. I know that. The couple down there among the flowers and friends probably doesn't yet. I didn't. How can you, when you're seventeen? Did I marry Harry to move back to Arkansas and take my old life back?

Why does anyone marry anyone? We have our narratives. "We just hit it off. We had so much in common": Barbie's plastic hand is posed to take Ken's arm, her other hand to hold a bouquet—the frozen image that has nothing to do with the actual slow series of leanings until we see the inevitable direction. There is the nudging in our bones that, at some point, says, "You need to procreate." Another that says, even before we know it's talking to us, "You'll need to get help for the difficult job of parenting." The more sophisticated one that says, "You'll want to get help from the mate most able to supply the best-quality offspring, the best-quality help." Alas, this sensible, rational one can easily be obscured by a deeper signal, one we can't hear, that responds to some limbic call, some primal emotional need that overwhelms good sense. No matter: we use our words. We call it choice. Harry came to Missouri over Thanksgiving and we bought rings. We married during his mid-semester break from his freshman year in college. We were so young our parents had to sign for us.

You could say the story behind my first wedding is the story of my life to that point. I wanted out of my family. Now, not later. Who was I? I was that resolute young woman who watched her mother sobbing in the kitchen. Whose mother sobbed, "What will I tell Nana?," her fear of her own mother greater than her awareness of her daughter's confused decision. Truly, my mother didn't know what to do. Life often felt like too much for her. She married a difficult man, and she had a seriously brain-damaged son to take care of. When I looked at her own wedding pictures, it seemed to me that the innocence on her face was terrifying.

So, no matter how she felt at the time, Mother took me to buy my long, white dress with its swarm of netting at the Buckner-Ragsdale department store. We picked out a veil that came halfway down my back. We ordered the three-layer cake. I was in for it now. I was way ahead of myself, breathless. I don't remember walking down the aisle. Oh, yes, now I'm there, fiercely determined. There are his Buddy Holly glasses, his slightly crooked teeth, the wave of his dark hair in front. Our cobbled-together bridal party of my new next-door neighbor, two high school friends from my hometown, and my sister. Oh, Lord, didn't I know even then it wasn't him I was marrying, but marriage?

This was 1962. You needed to get married if you wanted to have sex without fear. Pretty much. You needed to get married if you wanted a ticket to adult life. The bride's dress and her "going-away" dress were described in local newspapers, not just in the *New York Times*. That was me in our local paper. The usual lace and a few beads at the bodice. They always wrote that. And then a tan suit with a faint flower print on skirt and jacket. Heels. A clumsy but sincere facsimile of what a real, grownup wedding would look like, with its embossed invitations, beloved bridesmaids, meticulously planned reception. Many years later, when my sister and I cleared out my father's house, I took the wedding dress from its "forever box," and we took turns holding it up in front of us, snapping photos. I could have gotten into it, almost, except for the waist. What was so funny? It was a beautiful dress. The laughter was a turning away from sadness. I brought it to an antique store. "I'll take it," the owner said. "We have a demand for costumes for the college, for plays and Halloween and stuff."

Forty to fifty percent of marriages end in divorce. That knowledge tinges all weddings. Yet we plunge ahead, promising and meaning it, promising and crossing our fingers, promising and hoping. Who wrote this script? God? Mattel? What sort of script has the power to make a vow stick?

Christians call marriage one of the sacraments. They borrowed the word "sacrament" from the Roman Army. A recruit for the Roman army became a soldier by undergoing a *sacramentum*. He took an oath of office, got branded behind the ear, signifying new responsibilities and advantages. Latin theologians chose the word as the best Latin equivalent of the Greek word "mystery." A church rite is a mystery, "an outward and visible sign of an inward and invisible grace."

Take the Eucharist, for example, the heart of the Christian sacraments, the one in which tangible objects, wine and bread, become the body and blood of Christ. That's the word: "become." Whole wars have been fought about what that word means. Whole religions split off. "Belief" is a concept. Yet the act is enactment. If the "I" and the divine feel separate, the act itself is intended to refute that, over and over.

What's in their minds, the couple standing down there under the arch, saying their vows? The minister must be asking them to join hands. She smoothes the top layer of her dress and transfers her ribboned bouquet of domesticated wildflowers to her bridesmaid. Is she thinking about anything in particular? Is she trying not to think, but to hold this moment in her heart forever? Does the moment itself feel like forever to them? Do their vows feel like forever? The sacrament of marriage—according to the Catholic church, at least—is a vocation, a calling. I wonder if this young couple actually sees their marriage as the beginning of a whole new line of work.

Was I thinking of anything when I walked down the aisle with Harry? No matter. Like the couple below me, my body was enacting a ritual so old that what I thought about it was hardly relevant. I was doing it. Crossing a threshold that only exists because of the pressure of years, the ancient designations. That I was unconscious of the forces driving me, that I had, at my age, a still incompletely developed brain, didn't matter to the ritual. It never has. To step into ritual is to become the sacrifice, mind and body, that confirms the marriage of the act itself to whatever lies beyond meaning.

Literal, metaphoric—it's still about words. In the Roman Empire, the lower classes had "free" marriages. All it took was the bride's father delivering her to the groom, and the two would speak their mutual agreement that they were wed. But in wealthy families, when there was property at stake, documents would get signed listing property rights, and there would be a public declaration to assure that the marriage was legal, not common law.

When my younger sister got married, I was so unhappy in my own marriage that I stood there, her bridesmaid, red-faced, tears streaming. Embarrassing, but I couldn't quit. Someone quietly handed me a

Kleenex. Her vows and the ritual surrounding them cracked open my barely cemented-over anguish. I could see what I couldn't say. I could see what I had sacrificed: this kind of happiness. I felt like a sacrifice myself. I had been unconscious. I had led my own self to the slaughter.

The idea of sacrifice began, as language always does, literally, concretely. The first reported human sacrifice was the killing and skinning of the daughter of the king Cóxcox of Culhuacán. When the Franciscans insisted the Aztec priests cease their human sacrifices, the priests said, "Life is because of the gods; with their sacrifice they gave us life. . . . They produce our sustenance . . . which nourishes life." Everything on earth is *tonacayotl*—"spiritual flesh-hood." The Franciscans had come to promote a bloodless sacrifice. A substitute human. A substitute lamb. A gesture, embodied, of course, in the life of Christ. Simone Weil, who, despite being raised in a secular Jewish household and with no history of religious devotion, told a friend how, as she recited "Love," by George Herbert, "Christ himself came down and took possession of me."

"I learned it by heart," she said. "Often, at the culminating point of a violent headache, I make myself say it over, concentrating all my attention upon it and clinging with all my soul to the tenderness it enshrines. I used to think I was merely reciting it as a beautiful poem, but without my knowing it the recitation had the virtue of a prayer."

How can we not hear the wedding vows as both prayer and poem? How can we not be moved to tears?

I, _____, take thee, _____, to be my wedded Husband/Wife, to have and to hold from this day forward, for better for worse, for richer for poorer, in sickness and in health, to love and to cherish, till death us do part, according to God's holy ordinance.

"Till death do us part." Not "till death parts us." The simple reversal of words is the language of poetry, the language that sacrifices blind, direct sense for the stumble that provokes awareness. And "God's holy ordinance." And however we understand it, think how much of a lock this is: God being the highest authority imaginable, holy being the highest realm, and ordinance being the strongest prescription!

The words pick us up and carry us over the threshold. Though the crossing apparently is not necessarily permanent. The twelve years of my first marriage, when did they cease being a marriage? When did the gesture empty itself of meaning? It was a gesture filled with misgivings from early on, but patched and stitched until finally, undeniably, its fraying left more holes than cloth. Until the bitter end, the idea of marriage reigned over the reality of it.

What was the idea of it, anyway? *Take care of me. Be warm next to me. Keep me from being afraid. Get me out of my youth and into what people call adulthood.* The marriage of true minds seems true when your mind is so young and unformed that you can fit anywhere.

So I bought a long, white muslin dress, embroidered with multicolored flowers at sleeves, hem, and neckline. It was 1975, the graduate student world I was newly a part of still celebrating the arrival of the Age of Aquarius. We—the new we—wrote our own vows, another try (second for me, third for him) at getting it right. Our rings were carved with the flame in D. H. Lawrence's *Lady Chatterley's Lover*. My two children, eleven and six, stood at our sides, baffled, smiling. My decision had come so quickly. They barely knew him. I barely knew him. I knew he was darkly gorgeous. What underground stream sent me here, in this ultimately disastrous direction? How does it happen that the worst can come dressed as the best? For that matter, how can thousands of people believe in the person who seemingly will help them, when exactly the opposite is true? Jim Jones, Branch Davidians, Donald Trump, terrorists of all flavors—how is it that the search for truth and love sometimes seems to close our sense-gates instead of opening them? You fall in love with an image of who you want to fall in love with. You fall. You step into the ritual of bonding. You step, as if asleep. You may be asleep.

I say the vows, I make a promise, and unless my mind later changes its mind, my body is directed to adhere to the vows, to be faithful unto death. Isn't this how it's supposed to work? I am of two minds. I am of one mind. I am a mind. The mind, one supposedly imagines, can direct the body as if the body were only its witless, mechanical tool.

In 1991, I buy a simple off-white dress, street-length, that can be worn again. We—a new we—have been living together for almost two years, we've recently bought a house together, yet he goes to a motel overnight so we can meet at the church in a symbolic reenactment of virginity, or newness in general. We have only our grown children and a few friends to witness the event. We have not invited my parents or sisters, or his brothers. They scold us later, but this feels like our private affair. Mendelssohn's "Wedding March," a church full of people, and the throwing of rice, as far as we could see, had accomplished nothing. We are quietly married in the Episcopal church. We have, as required, met with our priest, who agrees to marry us in spite of our divorces. I cry in his office. I am terrified of doing this again. I want to do it wrapped in genuine church ritual, with as much protection as I can muster. Again. This time I pray my mind and my body are talking to each other in some meaningful way. I have had years of therapy.

That was twenty-seven years ago. We've been enacting this marriage for that long, surely forever now. Getting up every morning and making breakfast together. Fussing, arranging, kissing, and all the rest. We are more alike and more different than we used to be. Our pheromones have spoken to each other; our differences have rubbed like two stones, to a smoothness. Marriage may be all in the head, but it gradually diffuses into the very air in the room.

I was out for a walk, and came upon a wedding. I didn't know the couple. Still, I wanted to cry. Here we go again, I thought, as if they were the whole human race. Here we go plunging into what we don't understand, what will change us beyond our knowing. Here we go again, all this expense, preparation, all the history of language at our backs, to bring us to one short moment. No wonder we take so many pictures. It's hard to believe without them.

Bill's Clay Figures

1.

Okay, it does look like an elongated penis, but when you come closer, there are arms wrapped around, hands resting on hips, two heads melded—one turned one way, the other nestled against the taller one's neck. The clay is cracked all the way through midway down and again an inch above that. The nail through the bottom of the board is not enough support for the years it's been sitting on the shelf, one of several models for sculptures my friend Bill decided not to make. This one's not terribly original, not surprising, a bit like Giacometti in its elongation, interesting more for its unfinished brokenness, the bent house-nail obtruding at the slightly spread clay base.

The two figures lean slightly backwards, with grace and a Chagall-like fragility, a floaty feeling like stretching into love. You know: his painting "The Birthday," with the lover lifted off the floor, head turned back to kiss his darling, both of them fluid, unmoored in space. When I trace the outlines of these clay bodies, though, my finger catches on the ugly bits that have hardened without having been smoothed, a whitish cast to the more dried areas.

Still, it's something, to be held that way, to be the first slither of the sculptor's hands, when the mind is concerned only with the opening out, when the mind is utterly fastened to the hands.

It's the look of first love, when a person's gaze remains a long time on the beloved, and the looking itself is carried along like finger marks in clay, like tool marks that only slightly differentiate one figure from

the other. A particular density arises, forming what we knew before knowing. The excitement of norepinephrine and serotonin, the ease and float of dopamine. I've been in love like that, wandering the rooms of a dream castle, not to be confused with what comes later. These clay forms are made out of holding on, feet locked to a rough chunk of oak, the two hopeful heads all those inches above, keeping each other safe.

Or maybe it's not love. Maybe Bill was just playing with shapes. I think I am slightly perverse, bringing this piece of junk home from his studio, where I'd been discussing with him an entirely different project, where I turned idly to this cracked clay, this aborted effort, this seeming lover's cliché, nailed to a piece of grooved flooring, quick, clumsy, covered with dust.

I laugh at myself. Why am I always making something out of nothing? Why did I spend the evening in a parked car at Tilly Willy Quarry, with the hands and the kissing and the never-satisfied longing, imagining myself into the high pitch of marriage? Why do I keep running my hands over the rough edges of those first attempts, of the turning from home toward that dark-haired, skinny, Tareyton-smoking possibility, the one I believed could open my heart, take it in his hands and lift it into the air? We were in the steamed-up Buick, knowing nothing, all our knowing only wanting, all the wanting bigger than we were, already formed into some final shape far outside our moment, with no more bearing on that moment than completion has as it looks backward toward its source with a new kind of longing. Like a child sucking its thumb. Or an email from an old high school pal who lists with a rapturous attention the names of the old streets and the grid pattern they make.

I'm doing it again. I've looked for so many years at the particulars of longing, stared so intently at glittering store windows, that what I thought I wanted begins to vaporize. Maybe they were only reflections in the first place, my ideas of love. Meanwhile, there is this clay figure casting its shadow, carrying itself with the dignity of the doomed, willing to stand as long as it can, caring not at all about what I think.

2.

Inside me is this figure, hunched on its knees, arms pulled in, hands together not as in prayer, but turned out like flippers—yet not like flippers, but bent and touching only at the wrist, a bit fetal. You feel the movement of the sculptor's hands, his pinching together of the little body, his flattening of the ears, the hands. The head is merged with the neck and thrust forward like an ape's head, the scalp a series of rough tool-scrapes. One eyebrow's cocked, the other overhanging like an ape's—this poor tense human, this helpless ape, this made thing.

It's not easy to be anything. The shoulders want to curve inward, so out of love are they with themselves. They have seen the worst. They've watched the seagulls invent confidence and have winced. They are my friend Bernie who will never leave New Jersey, never leave Metuchen, not even his townhouse, if he can help it. What is wrong with Bernie? He said if he ever got tenure, it would kill him, and that was true. He wrote a novel about a man who could never leave Metuchen. It's really good, but it sits in a drawer, unpublished. Also, my father told me that when he was young, he would see a very nice lady friend of his mother's coming across the bridge and he'd duck under, crawl through high brush to avoid having to say hello. Our theories of incapacity are made up of energy waves only. They are like mosquitoes we could brush away. We think up our own feet of clay.

I used to meditate cross-legged, but my knees gave out, so now I use a bench with a soft Dacron zabuton under my knees. Bill's figure and I are both praying with no words. We can't get out of the prayer until we're broken apart. That is, I have a cerebral cortex that is able to turn back on itself and see itself in action, which is a constant prayer. When I say "broken apart," I see the frozen bay in late March, cracking, a small galaxy of itself now beginning to float on itself. And I realize that nothing gets away, so I take back what I said about getting out of prayer.

Suppose it were snowing like crazy, huge piles of it accumulating. Or maybe there would be cherry blossoms that look like snow. "Loveliest of trees, the cherry now / Is hung with bloom along the bough," goes the Housman poem. On a website devoted to explications of poems, someone wrote that "the persona wants to say that as long as we're still young we have to do something good and see how God creates our beautiful world." Isn't this prayer, the way she shapes the poem to be what she wants, making it look like the inside of her own mind? Letting it loop and feed back?

This figure has serious haunches, which are their own feedback. They interview the body to see how much of it needs to be held up. Here Bill has made two balls of clay and pushed them together enough to make them hold. From the back you can see the nail they're impaled upon. The nail makes me nervous, which shows how much I am able to be this guy, how much I understand his hurt. I could tell you whole stories, but try instead to see the actually graceful lines of this figure: from head to hunched shoulders to those small flipper-arms to the hips rolled outward and the legs tucked back. Imagine a question mark. Imagine a question mark built on a nail. It would look like a dollar sign, or a treble clef. Imagine the nail coming all the way up and protruding a tiny bit, like a tuft on a beanie cap, from the top of the head. That will give you an idea of the loneliness of humans, of which I am one.

I should mention that the nail, or the shrinkage of clay over time, has raised the figure so that he isn't even touching his board, He floats almost a half-inch above it. I'd say he's aware of the miraculous nature of his position, given his half-smile, his actually kind-of-thoughtful smile. He may have figured out that he is the inside of Bill's mind and is experiencing the bliss of having given his life over to his creator. Or he has realized that he can do nothing else, which is the same thing.

3.

Remember how your classmates bent their arms at the elbow, rested their hands on their rib cages, and flapped like chickens? Squawk,

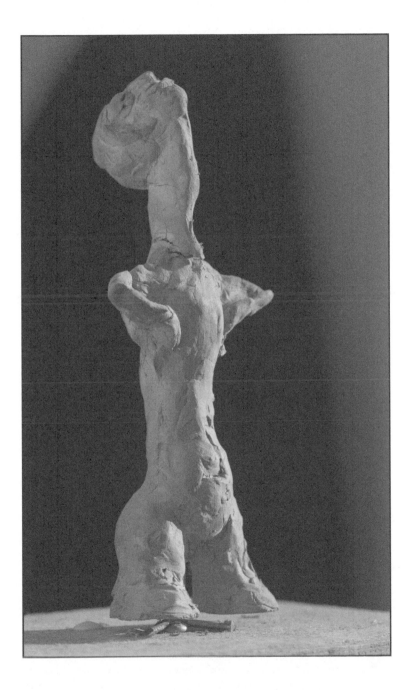

squawk, you chicken. You coward. You of faint wing, incapable of sustained flight. Stupid chicken, so stupid you'd drown yourself looking up in a rainstorm. And after the perfect ones were finished with their litany, sometimes their victim would look up, head turned upward into the rain of language, arms bent like a chicken's wings, and smile.

Bill's figure is smiling, even if the dried clay makes the smile look a little like nearsighted Mr. Magoo's. The smile here is one of knowing better. Bill's figure would like to offer his very large Adam's apple, he would like to offer his neck like Saint Paul, Saint Luke. His chin tilts upward as if he were about to take off and fly away. God knows he's tried. Rain could be pouring onto his face like the stones upon Saint Peter. Isn't he well aware of the host of martyrs behind him, those who stood like this? Wasn't it like this? Whoever knows if the course one dreams, one chooses, is right?

The body itself is a dream, each facet proportioned, enlarged or shrunken, according to where the mind chooses to turn its attention. Imagine moving a magnifying glass around over the body. Where is this small figure's mind? It seems to be on his torso, reaching; on his heart, giving over. He is made with the foolish disproportion of a martyr concentrated on one idea, elfin little legs not leaving their spot. The two silver nails that hold him are clearly visible at the crotch. In a sense, he died before he began: Bill had already fastened him down before the body could muster up a thought of its own. What silliness. A subject has arisen, a figure has arisen. I don't know if they have anything to do with each other.

What is the point of trying to exist like a god? The god is singing descant; all we can do is improvise. Fault and slip, clay and tool, this figure's navel is dug out with one small motion as if its body were thus detached from its source.

Let us forgive ourselves for taking on a form that can only lead to failure. In 1777, Mozart composed his Piano Concerto No. 9 in E-flat Major, interjecting a soloist into the first movement and a slow minuet section in the third, failing over and over to move in the expected direction. Alfred Brendel called it "one of the greatest wonders of the world."

This is only one example of what can happen when the ear thinks one thing is coming but something else emerges, every strand unpredictable.

Likewise, the Mozart platform for distributed computer programming separates the components of a program to avoid easy, predictable speech between them. So, if one part of a global internet structure fails, the various channels are closed off from each other, to maintain security or prevent damage in some other part of the system. The Mozart failure model defines what failures are recognized by the system and how they are reflected in the system's language.

Let us forgive ourselves for our obsession with perfection, for our vague sense of what that might be. In search of some transcendent understanding, I have left Bill's figure standing with his little arms cocked, announcing his completion. He's done. His form is his form. When I turn back, he ignores me, chin in the air. We are at this point utterly simpatico, each of us transferring our energy to the other for no reason, two burning bushes.

4.

I'm not sure if this one is a single figure sitting on the ground, bent forward and using its arms for support, or if this is two figures, one directly behind the other and attached to the other's back. Moister clay on top of drier clay might be giving the appearance of two, but looking at the hump behind the first one's head and the seeming doubling of the arms, I'm inclined to think there *are* two. Actually, this piece is barely anything, just a start. Kind of a sad start, too, she (I imagine this) leaning her head on his back in sympathy. What is this great weight of soul?

Selah.

I examine the photos of my mother after she married my father. They are on a beach. Her hair blows back, wild and curly, and she looks at

the camera with an impish sexiness, aware of her beauty. I can hardly follow the photos forward to the other, the bent and sad person. I know her weight of soul, what it was made of—or at least as well as I can. I would remove that weight, if I could.

Yet when I begin unthreading the components, one by one, I am left with only a handful of thread. *Selah.* The night she died (I always come back to that), my father, my sisters, and I were sleeping or lying awake at her house with our eyes toward the ceiling at the very moment her breath stopped. The nurse had called from the hospital, but my father thought we could wait until morning. Look at how I return to the pain, the guilt that feels like an emptiness. "I like a look of Agony, / Because I know it's true," says Emily Dickinson.

I do not know why Bill didn't follow through and make a large sculpture out of this small draft. I love the curve of the bodies, the duplication of arms, the bend of the head somewhere between prayer and resignation. The peace of the back figure resting against the other. *Selah.*

The word "selah" is found particularly in Psalms, but in other books of the Old Testament as well. It's probably a liturgical musical mark, a musical strum. Thirty-one of the thirty-nine psalms containing the phrase "to the choir-master" also include the word "selah." It appears to be an instruction on the reading of the text, like "Stop and listen" or "Let those with eyes see and with ears hear." Sometimes the word functions like "amen," stressing the importance of the preceding passage. Sometimes it seems to mean "forever." Another interpretation claims that "selah" comes from the primary Hebrew root word *calah*, which means "to hang"—by implication to measure (weigh), to measure against.

Psalms 4:4. Stand in awe, and sin not: commune with your own heart upon your bed, and be still. Selah.

Psalms 9:20. Put them in fear, o LORD: that the nations may know themselves to be but men. Selah.

Psalms 57:6. They have prepared a net for my steps; my soul is bowed down: they have digged a pit before me, into the midst whereof they are fallen themselves. Selah.

In the first example, there is a strumming; in the second, *harken*; in the third, more of an *amen*, or *forever*. But they're all open to interpretation. In any case, the need for rest is there, the marking of rest. As in Bill's figures, as in this one in particular: bent down and facing the ground, unable at the moment to do more.

My grandson Jake, when he was only nine, stood on the end of the dock, looking back at the poplar tree. "I like to see the negative space around things," he said, having read all of *Harry Potter*. Sometimes a person wants to tune the ear to the rests, too—in music, in poetry—instead of just to the notes or the words. You hear the blackened bar, or the white space, that causes the whole to be itself. First there was my mother with her hair in the breeze. *Selah.* Then there are those other photos. I wonder, when we make a shape—out of clay or words or whatever—if we're mostly hearing the silences, trying to bring the edge of our imagination as close as possible to the edge of the silence, and behold, in the space between, it turns out there was a shape that we've now made visible.

5.

Isn't this what we want, finally—to be like this figure? Isn't this how we position ourselves for the Christmas card photo? People so close together that our only separations are as small as these pale channels dug into clay. Five figures here, their arms wrapped around behind each other. A tiny family, the tallest member only about seven inches, but each stretched tall and holding its head angled to show how closely they're all pulling toward each other. Their combined bodies make a flowing skirt of clay that extends to the support nails at their base. Nails bent over and around each other as if they were all chained together.

And the nails emerge, too, from the tops of their heads, as if supports for halos now missing. You know those primitive-looking clay rings of people holding hands, the kind sold in gift stores, sometimes with candles, symbolizing a marketable variety of unity, of love? This is a bit like that, I'm afraid, except for the roughness, the bare tool-scrapes, the dried-out and shrunken clay. They're huddled by themselves, a small windbreak against the worst, a tenderness born of fragility and imperfection. They are so thin. How am I any different from the shoppers in gift stores, the way I've carried these models home from Bill's studio in a cardboard box, breaking my neck to make metaphor out of them? Speaking for the speechless, finishing what was unfinished in Bill's head, taking hold of his once-elastic thought and pulling it until it nearly breaks, worrying that thought the way I worry a rough fingernail.

✳   ✳   ✳

What does Bill do all day every day out there in his studio in the woods, the woodstove going, his small radio playing? He is rolling a towel to block the cold air from under the door; he is turning his utility lights toward the new work. He is ruffling his gray hair and pulling his cap back down. He is cleaning off his pick, sawing a piece of plywood; he is dabbing paint, lighting his torch for the metal figures. He is not making a living. He is not getting famous. He is fastening shapes together without giving preliminary thought to the issue of meaning. His soul is like his figures.

And where is the soul, anyway? When the nail points upward, does it lead the soul toward or away from its home? Does the narrative depend upon who's telling it? I'm telling this story. If it is not a good story, that's my fault. If I reach the end of my imagination, that's my fault. There is Bill in his studio, here are his first tries in front of me. I am desperate to carry them to some successful conclusion. I, who have always worked hard.

I must change my life. When Rilke stared his minutes and hours at the archaic torso of Apollo, he had to give up his old way of seeing. After all, the head was missing, the part that would have been able to look back at him. There was only the body, and it turned out the body required a loosening of the gaze, the participation of the entire life of the looker. Because when there is no way to exchange a look, when there is none of the language possible that sometimes can get us out of these awkward situations by shifting cleverly from phrase to phrase, we must call upon all we know. And yet we fail. There is only us. There was only Rilke. And the torso. He tried a poem, but the poem was only more clever conversation, a last-ditch effort. The space between them was like the permanent space between Michelangelo's outstretched fingers: God to Adam, Adam to God. It was the main event—this holding apart, this not knowing.

Mirrored Transoms

Our neighbor has been renovating her condo for almost a year. Just cosmetic changes, she said, but the place has been gutted, the hundred-year-old chair rails and trim are gone. Now there are all sorts of soft gray built-ins, floors stained fashionably dark, wallpaper, and so on. I know because we live next door and I poke my head in from time to time to fret over what the workmen are doing.

It took me weeks to see what's been done to the high transom windows (our ceilings are eleven feet high) over the doors and the front entryway. I kept thinking there were lights on in there, but one day I just stood and looked. I got a flashlight and shone it on the windows. The light bounced back at me. She'd had them covered with mirrors! What I'd been seeing was the lit hallway.

If I stood on a ladder, I'd be seeing myself.

I can't help looking up every day as I pass, harboring a vague sense of being shut out. A general sense of a soft glimmer at the junction of what I can and can't know. I wish I had words for this feeling.

Not exactly a glimmer. More like a thought that travels past the boundary, past the gravitational field, and thins outward until some distant source sends it back to you. More like the way you see a creek running under grasses when the sun hits it. Oh, there it is! Like when I head out for a walk behind our historic buildings, along the warren of trails up on the hill. I'm exploring, in a sense, another world: this summer a peace sign woven of vines hung from one of the trees. Who put it there? Who took it down? The flat old water tank in the woods is decorated with amazingly skillful graffiti, overlaid so thick on the old graffiti, the whole is a blast of cartoon-fat signatures and designs from the secret world of teenagers, of gentle insurrectionists.

The path is soggy these days, leaves making the slopes, especially the rocks, slippery. Where the trail dips down into the cedars, the broken-down organic matter is black as tar and clings to my shoes. It is secret and dark in here. Now I am "in here." Wherever else my thoughts have gone, when I reach this stretch, I am entirely here. Alien and muddy, at the lowest spot.

There is something crucial about this: wandering to the low point, as if I have to feed on it. There are no words there, but that's probably the point. I have to stare into that, and later, the words are never right, but I have to try. There was my cancer, then the words for it, then words for me ("fear," "sorrow"), and then the wordlessness beneath the words.

The same feeling from high up instead of low, when Jerry and I were standing on the Cliffs of Mohr—cocooned up there, same as cocooned down there, for a few minutes, a strange and looser attachment to the mundane earth. The whipping wind—and my mind then turns to our condo, on the third floor. When the wind blows—as it does particularly hard off Grand Traverse Bay a few blocks away—the sound is eerie, otherworldly. Our huge building used to be the Northern Michigan State Asylum. I can imagine the mental patients living here long ago, hearing the sound of wild, uncontrollable spirits, trying to eat, dress, bathe, with the spirits raging in their ears.

Everything I write eventually bumps into that mirror. When I can't see any farther, there goes my mind, taking on the problem. When I was a child, at our lake there was Old Dave, who lived in a little house not a quarter mile up what's now called Woody Knoll Road. We walked all the way to the top picking wild blackberries for Old Dave, we said, wanting an altruistic reason for the picking. When our buckets were full, we walked back down and timidly knocked on his door. Very scary, a bearded old man in a ragged flannel shirt in the middle of summer. Inside his house it was dark, with magazine pages stuck on the walls from the Joe Louis/Max Schmeling fight. He'd thank us for the berries and tell us about the fight, which he remembered in detail from the radio.

Now I can tell you that Joe Louis was the most important Black athlete of his age, a focal point for Black pride in the 1930s. Schmeling represented Nazi Germany. Against the backdrop of the Great Depression, the fights stood for the struggle between democracy and fascism. I can tell you that in the first fight, Louis was knocked out. Old Dave's magazine pages were probably of the rematch. The poet Maya Angelou, who listened to the fight over the radio in her uncle's country store in rural Arkansas, said that when Louis was on the ropes, "My race groaned. It was our people falling. It was another lynching, yet another black man hanging on a tree. . . . It would all be true, the accusations that we were lower types of human beings. Only a little higher than the apes."

And then he won. Bands, dancing in the streets. How did Old Dave feel? Where was he then? Not in his little house, but at the top of the hill in the old Airstream trailer that's turned on its side now, the one I used to explore, where I took away a cup, an old coffee pot, as souvenirs. Like Old Dave, I collect artifacts and press into them as far as I can.

Now I can tell you that his family moved him down the hill so that they could bring him food in the winter. He was a little crazy. He was a hermit. We children called him a hermit, loving that word. What did we know of a hermit? What does any of us know? Only that he—or she—exists at the bottom, or in a cave at the top. We don't know how to understand someone who won't conform. So we bring him berries. Sometimes we think he's a sort of god, because he seems to need nothing but himself. His mind furnished pictures enough to make him content, so it seemed.

The stone foundation of his house is still there, on Woody Knoll Road, in the front yard of a newer house and planted with flowers. I've thought of him often. Some neighbors at the lake know his history, his family. I have not asked very many questions because each answer seems to flatten the story, deflate my imagination. The work of the imagination is to press on, beyond the barrier of facts. Not to ignore facts, not to discredit them, but to see through them into the space where the separations into here and there, then and now, are no longer the point.

The management company for our condo association has sent our neighbor a letter, chastising her for what she's done to the historic space, although there's not much that can be changed now. The mirrors are clever, though, and I commend her for that solution for privacy. Jerry and I argue a bit about this. He is an eighteenth-century scholar and lover of all things historical. He doesn't like it when people mess with history. He's studied and written about the history of the novel, starting with Cervantes's *Don Quixote* in 1605 and springing to a wide and popular genre in the eighteenth century. The modern novel is intimate, private. You can burrow into its secret life. The novel—as is true for visual art, for all art—began as gesture, as mimic of "real" life, as close to a mirror image as possible. A play, onstage, on the stage of the mind. After photography, after the splitting of the atom, after the big wars, when art began to turn inward, the direction of seeing reversed itself. Instead of mirroring the objective world, it was our own minds we thought we saw in the mirror—the textural excitement of Van Gogh, the balletic distortions of Matisse, the multiple angles of Picasso.

Our section of the building, we've been told, housed the seriously crazy patients. The whole huge complex was designed to allow patients to work, meet, socialize, in as attractive and supportive an environment as possible. Yet our section was a locked ward. I sometimes sit in our bedroom, which is also my study, and try to imagine what it was like to be a patient here, hearing the wind howl, the mind turned back on itself so that all it knows is the story it makes up, full of demons and spirits.

Spirits, being weightless, float upward. Demons are heavy, downward-urging. The concrete floors on the lower level of our quarter-mile-long building sit over joining tunnels, tunnels higher than your head, rounded at the bottom, arched at the top, the same way the Romans built them. Before the renovation, kids used to sneak in and wander through, smoking, drinking, listening to their echoes. A forbidden zone. Tunnels used to connect all the buildings. Nurses, doctors, and workers could walk through them, and steam and water pipes, electrical conduits, were bracketed to the walls. Some were shafts to pull fresh air throughout the hospital and out the spires on top. An ecosystem, a cosmos, literally a bricks-and-mortar version of Dante's universe.

Or of *Paradise Lost*, maybe. The height and depth and breadth of Milton's cosmos was the height and depth and breadth of his mind, of the minds of the prophets, added together, so dense they curved space to make a safe enclosure.

Across the huge lawn from us is Willow Cottage Assisted Living, one of the other renovated buildings on this 480-acre campus, where my father lives now. The residents there are pretty much safely contained within their own ecosystems. Sweetly, for the most part. If they were hostile, they'd live somewhere else. Their minds have grown less limber, less able to maneuver in the outer world. So the front door opens with a code, the stairway doors with a different one. But even for us, who are still agile in that way, the stories we tell ourselves about what's true can easily admit no external world. That's what crazy means, isn't it?

For the patients in the locked ward, there is only the present. For those who live as external a life as possible, the sober fact of death can be held in a locked closet for a long while. Until a diagnosis, for example. Yet, with or without our permission, the moment of death brings the interior and exterior to the threshold together.

My father has said for years he wants to die. But, really, his talk about it is his way of warding it off. He's afraid. No point in trying to examine why. I know how it is, since my cancer. Isn't it sane, after all, to dread seeing our great good fortune of being born human, intelligent, and capable come to an end? Others at Willow Cottage sleep their way slowly toward their end. Others forget who they are, so fear doesn't know where to lodge.

Mother officially died from choking on a piece of Halloween candy. She'd been having ministrokes all along, so probably she had a stroke as she was chewing. By the time I got to the hospital from halfway across the country, she was lying there unable to speak. But when her three daughters gathered around her and bent down to kiss her, tears ran out of her eyes. The MRI soon after showed no brain activity. I thought many times about her fear of the enclosure of the MRI and imagined that she was still alert enough to feel that fear. I wondered what she felt when we were gathered in her room, waiting for death. She seemed unaware, but the nurse came in and shouted in her ear, "I'm going to aspirate your throat, Mrs. Brown, so you can breathe better." The nurse turned to us and said, "They can sometimes hear, you know." I keep that image with me, the trouble in my mind about what my mother knew and didn't know, when she fully crossed the threshold and what I might have done or said at that moment that could have held her gently in the passage.

Not that I ever knew my mother, not really. I've tried to see into her and my heart hurts. She was battered by a life she didn't know how to get out of or fix. She was kind and gentle. And cheerful by nature. When she threw herself across the bed in tears, she would recover like a child, with little residue of sadness. Or is that what I'd like to think? I had to ignore her suffering so I could grow up, myself. That's what it felt like. It felt as if, had I been inside her mind, I would have died of sorrow.

Do unto others. I wanted to be good, and kind. I was offered that conduit between heaven and earth that Sunday school provided. I lifted mine eyes unto the hills and tried desperately to see beyond. To live beyond. I sat in a tiny chair in a semicircle with the others and sang "What a Friend We Have in Jesus" to the flat notes of the piano. This was the group worship session with words read out of the booklet. Then our individual classes, where we trekked through the bible stories, week by week. If we weren't sure what to make of them, the moral was printed at the bottom of the page. What was soaking into us during those years, those of us who were faithful?

We prayed. Sat in a circle and bowed our heads in submission to Something Greater Than Ourselves. Something separate that we needed to reach. That's what I thought; that's what we thought. As if the thing greater were not located inside ourselves. As if there were anything separate from anything. Everything felt separate. My small athletic body, restless; my nose, with its own separate awareness of the musty smell of the wooden floors, the old classroom; my fingers playing with the pages that held each week's scripture, plus a prayer; my ears, tuning in and out. I was only marginally a believer by nature. I had inherited my father's atheism in my rational brain, but there was also my mother's irrational belief in something else, something called "out there." Called "Greater" by the Sunday school booklet. By the minister.

What was my Sunday school teacher thinking? How did her belief work? When her mind bumped against the unknowable, did it move on out into space, or did it stop at the border and turn back, turn the page, and read to us what was written there. Look, these words stand for what I don't know. But the words know. They are words, and they must know something.

There was Bessie, who taught the adult women's class, had taught it for years. One morning she got up, went to church, taught her class, came home, ate dinner, took a nap, and died. I have thought about this as a good life, a good death. And then I think, I don't know. Is this life any better than the drunk's, the criminal's? What if the criminal sees the truth and can't get to it, keeps trying, by all the twisted routes he knows? Through whose eyes is there a judgment? Is there a point of reference out there that doesn't shift, that is the same now and forever? And what about the person whose last moments are filled with pain and anguish that aids the leaving in some crucial way? We can't know.

Who can fathom death? I ask this in all earnestness, as I've come up against it myself. But, then, who can fathom birth? Ovum, sperm, an explosion of cells, each marked to build its portion of the structure. Then here comes the spark of life, out of nowhere, and the human mind that learns to say, "This is life." Learns to mirror itself.

Our great water, Grand Traverse Bay, is often glassy-smooth this season, late into the winter with no snow. When it finally comes, and it will, I'm sure, the surface will cloud over with ice. Below the ice will be walleye, pike, and perch, and the fishermen will set up their huts, cut holes through, bring their kerosene heaters and beer, and sit there for hours, leisurely fathoming what might swim up to their bait. Imagining. Their minds will be a mirror of their desire.

And I will be imagining them in their ice houses and writing what I think goes on there. What is their cryptic male conversation? Are they retelling fish tales? I have one for them.

My grandson Zach was fishing from the pontoon boat, way up the Chain of Lakes. He was ten, I think. The water was very clear. He saw northern pike down there, hovering, as they do, huge submarines. Then the jerk on his line and oh, lord, the fish to contend with, the terror of its rising with its prehistoric teeth, out of the other world, bent on destruction or return. Zach, his face gone white, pulled against the fearful thing, pulled until at last the line snapped. Shaky with relief, he looked down at the water reeds swaying, the fish gone already, the tale beginning to form in the absence of flesh.

Absence is a grand palette. When we moved in here, the huge, wide halls had nothing on the walls. Now we have art. This year it's multi-colored abstract paintings, with pieces of brightly colored wood planks and branches attached. A pleasure to see every time I walk down the hall. But ever since I figured out the mirrored transoms, my eyes turn to them instead. They're as fascinating as the paintings, the sculpture in the elevator foyer, the boots outside other people's condos. They can't look back at me because they're too high. I can't see myself. The light is a soft shimmer, almost like a window, but you can tell it isn't quite. And there's a slight telltale reflection of the wood trim at the sides. Not absence; not presence. It's enticing in a spooky way. Not a metaphor for anything, really, but still, I feel a bit floaty when I look up. Nothing is what it seems, and maybe I'm not, either.

Your Father, My Father: Volleys

For Judith Kitchen, pioneer in creative
nonfiction and my friend (1941–2014).

I t's already dark and picking up a slight chill, which feels pretty
good after the warm August day. We're sitting outside the Northern Pacific Coffee Company in Tacoma, Washington, at a tiny
wrought-iron table, drinking wine after an evening of readings at our
MFA residency. We're entertaining Linda Bierds, our master class poet
this year, and a few others with stories about our fathers. Judith's father
is dead. Fleda's is ninety-two. How did this get started? Something
about being a skinflint.

1. Razors

Fleda: A neighbor my father's age here at the lake told me that one
time my father sheepishly admitted to him that he didn't know anything about brands of razor blades, because he'd been using the same
one for years. He'd strop it every day on an old piece of leather. I
don't remember that. What I do remember is his rubbing a double-
sided blade on the inside of a drinking glass every day to sharpen it.
He'd slide it up and down with one finger, keeping exactly the right
pressure to hold the blades at an angle against the side of the glass. It
worked, the glass, I suppose, being tougher than the thin metal blade.
The only reason he shaved, he claimed, was to get my mother to kiss

him. Maybe in her honor, after she died, he continued using an electric razor she'd bought him, for a present, against his protest. When it died, he turned to the one my mother had used on her legs. It left large uneven patches on his chin and face so that he looked like he'd been shaved by a blind man.

Judith: Every summer, for the two weeks we were on vacation, my father didn't shave. My mother hated that almost as much as she hated the fact that he insisted she leave behind her plastic dish drainer because, if we were going to camp, he was supremely capable of lashing a drainer for us. After we had set up the tent, he sent us off to look for some "straight sticks" he could use, and by the time we returned he had managed to lash some longer poles between two trees. He then carefully placed our sticks at regular intervals and fastened them down with twine. "Just perfect," he'd announce. And he wouldn't hear any complaints—even when the dishes fell through the uneven spaces between the sticks. In the end, we had to dry the dishes with the towels my mother had packed, and the drainer became the place we stretched the towels to dry.

2. Presents

Judith: When I was little, whenever my father came back from a trip, he gave me a present—always the same thing: the tiny bar of soap from his hotel room or the train. One Christmas, he gave my mother a bouquet of plastic flowers that she pretended to like, and then he bought plastic flowers for the next seven years. For many years before he died, his Christmas present to each of us consisted of the free calendar he'd received from his bank. He also began to give what he called "generic" gifts—books from his shelves that he wrapped in newspaper and told us to trade until we all had the one we wanted most. At some time, he simply stopped buying shoes. Shirt cardboard, he said, did a good job of protecting the foot from water after a shoe had holes in the sole. And it could be easily replaced! That was because, neatly stored in his drawers, were all the presents we had given him. Shirt after shirt, ready to be plundered for its cardboard backing. The shirts themselves could wait while he worked at wearing out the ones he already owned.

Fleda: After my mother died, my father came to our house for Christmas. Feeling some pressure to participate in our gift exchange, he drew my husband's name and bought him a roll of Scotch tape, wrapped the best he could. Since then, we've all gotten a small card, signed, as is typical of his letters, with a typed "Phillips," "Dad" handwritten below it. My father hates gifts as much as he hates tipping in restaurants—at the same obligatory "generosity." He angrily chews his tongue when he's been given something he doesn't "need." On Christmas mornings, he would leave in the middle of gift opening to go down to check the furnace to make sure the valve he had just oiled hadn't gotten stuck again. He's willed his body to the University of Missouri medical school, not as a gift, but as a nose-thumbing to the funeral industry. He worries that if the medical school can't use it, he might accidentally be embalmed before we can put a stop to it.

3. Couture

Fleda: My father's father was an old-fashioned academic who wore a vest and tie most of the time; his mother had a quite smart wardrobe; his sister had hoped to be a fashion buyer for Marshall Field's. My father, however, possesses two pair of khaki pants and maybe three shirts, which he rotates until they thin to a vapor. He plans to make sure that he and his clothes wear out at the same time. His pants are stained with grease from changing the oil in his car and from stray dabs of glue or paint, since he scorns the idea of separating good and everyday wear. He found a two-dollar brown UPS uniform jacket at Goodwill and has been wearing it now for years. He wears the same bent-up brown utility shoes for hiking, changing the oil, digging out in the snow, and taking his lady friend (under duress) out to dinner. The soles are worn slick, so he has to be careful when it's wet outside. Sometimes he's glued on pieces of rubber, like retreading a tire, when they develop holes. He uses iron-on patches on his pants, whatever color's available, even if they don't match. To make sure they stay, he sews as well as irons them on, using any color thread available.

Judith: My father's claim to fame was Bermuda shorts. From the minute they came in, he took to them, though he never wore the requisite argyle knee socks. Since he was a redhead, he had terribly white skin covered with freckles and reddish hair. Shortly after my mother's death, we took him, along with his brother, my uncle Willy, to Toronto. We were hoping to distract him from his grief. My father wore Bermuda shorts. They were clean, neatly pressed, as always, but my uncle Willy was indignant that my father's knees were so "ugly." He sputtered in the elevator ride to the hotel room. A short, somewhat pudgy man, Uncle Willy bought almost all his clothes at Goodwill and, since most of the waists that fit him belonged to longer legs, he'd discovered a good way to shorten pants—staples. The trouble was, they rusted when the pants were washed, so he'd taken to rarely, if ever, doing laundry. Why he was miffed about my father's knees, I'll never really understand. Neither did my father, who recounted the story of the elevator long after Willy, too, had died.

4. Lady Friends

Judith: My father always claimed he had had to choose between two women when he decided to get married. He'd selected my mother because she had the better "sense of play." Certainly my parents had parties, ones we watched lying on the floor upstairs and peering down through the banister. Laughter floated upward, but all we could really see was shoes, pantlegs, and the hems of the somewhat fancy dresses. Since most of their friends were my father's scientific colleagues and their wives, the men tended to group together to talk, and the women did what wives were expected to do—compared children's accomplishments and talked about recipes.

These were intelligent women, most of them wives met at graduate school, but the 1940s and 1950s had driven them underground. They ran the PTAs and there was the occasional assistant to the dentist husband, or a librarian, a teacher, even one pediatrician. But, for the most part, they were "wives." So it was only after my mother's death that my father surprised us. First, by proposing, within two weeks, that the doctor's widow should marry him right away. Assuming this was a response to grief, she turned him down. After that, he ran through a series of the widows of his friends. Finally, he settled on a woman named Bonnie Butcher—someone we knew only as the mother of one of our classmates in high school. Bonnie was, for want of a better word, "flouncy"; her hair was dyed, her clothes were dramatic, and she owned a poodle that always sported a tiny bow to match her outfit on the top of its head. I decided to ask my father just what it was he saw in Bonnie. His reply: "When we walk into a restaurant, everyone looks up."

Fleda: After my mother died, I introduced my father to the senior center and warned him that he'd have casserole ladies lined up at his door in no time. It didn't take him long to cull one from the pack. The others all expected something of him, he said—to be supported, or at least to have some small cash investment in the relationship. But there was Lois, who was willing to put up with Sunday dinner at Friendly's and would split the cost of the meals they cooked together. She liked sex, the numero-uno criterion for my father. They've gotten along fine for years, now, having lunch together at the senior center, going to my father's house for dinner, having a "nap," then he drives her home. Home now for her is assisted living. Earlier, after Lois's heart attack, she lived with her daughter Maria, who decided she hated my father with a passion. No wonder. He dresses like a street bum, he sometimes smells, he chews with his mouth open. He never buys her gifts. And, clearly, he was having sex with Lois but wasn't proposing marriage. He used to bring her to the lake in the summers. One summer she seemed to be more disoriented than usual. My father wrote Maria one of his usual overwhelmingly detailed letters (didn't call) that suggested the apocalypse. Maria and her husband drove all the way from southern Missouri to northern Michigan to get Lois, who could have easily been seen by a local doctor. Once, when Lois was sick and my father wasn't allowed to visit, he wrote a letter that he fortunately let me read and veto. He compared his position with Lois's family to the relationship of the West to Kim Il Jong, the totalitarian leader of North Korea.

5. Collecting

Fleda: My father collects rubber bands, paper clips, screwdrivers. He has a large shoebox full of tire weights fallen from passing cars that he draws from occasionally to balances his own tires. He does this with a rig he invented—a Coke bottle with a circle of plywood on the top with a nail through it. He balances the tire on the nail and adds weights as appropriate. He also collects combs he picks up in the street. He has a shoebox full of those, all sizes and colors, as well as a shoebox full of used toothbrushes. He has copies of old *Harvard Reviews* (they come free, for a lifetime). The only magazine he subscribes to is *National Geographic*. His junk mail piles up on the floor, the dining table, the top of the eight-track player, the hutch. In his basement is the first bike I ever had, a used one—the only bike I ever had, for that matter—painted blue in 1953 to cover some slight rust, the crib my brain-damaged brother used from 1953 to 1960, colored aluminum cups, empty peanut butter jars, a freezer containing meat my mother put there before she died in 1995. And there are five or six plastic dishpans full of pieces of wire, electrical adaptors, an odd spoon, greasy rags, a rubber glove, electrical tape, rotting pieces of rope, chunks of wood in various shapes—all dark with oil or grease, with fingerprints.

   Judith: Talk about peanut butter jars. Their best use was for sorting nails. First, my father nailed the lids of the jars, thread side down, to a large beam in the ceiling of the cellar just over his workbench. Then he arranged the jars in a row on the bench and began sorting nails—first according to size. When he had a jar or two full of one particular size, he would spill them out again into a plastic dishpan and begin sorting according to degrees of rust. There was, in his mind, no category that would consign a nail to the dustbin. Then he'd carefully screw the jars into their lids. The ceiling was a sea of glass jars, glittering in the glare of the bare bulbs. Where did he get the nails? Well, from earlier projects that he'd dismantled, naturally. And this, of course, meant that he also had a collection of lumber stacked according to size and type of wood. He hardly had to use his saw because he could always find something the size he needed. Let's not get into the lead pipes, also sorted—by length and diameter. Suffice it to say, lead pipes do not make good legs for a ping-pong table.

6. Eating

Fleda: My father eats with his mouth open, chewing loudly. He chooses to stuff his mouth full especially before he speaks. The food often dribbles out the side as he makes a point. His parents gave and attended dinner parties. I used to think his eating habits were a deliberate disavowal of his parents, but I've come to recognize his true and deep unconsciousness. He eats like a three-year-old child, and when anyone, such as me, mentions his manners, he gets furious. "I don't tell YOU how to eat," he says. His habits of saving carry over here—he's gotten sick more than once by eating spoiled food in his refrigerator. If green beans have been there for two weeks, well, just cook them longer and they'll probably be okay. He has bags and jars of unidentifiable food in his freezer, some from when my mother was alive, fourteen or so years ago. My mother, unlike her mother-in-law, was an unimaginative cook, so my father sometimes took it upon himself to extend the menu on his own, cooking and canning the boysenberries that grew outside one house we rented, buying tongue (because it was cheap) and plopping it whole into the pressure cooker. It tasted like bitter shoe leather. He did grow lovely and elegant tomatoes, peppers, and green beans in his garden. I would wake up hearing him whistling through the rows early summer mornings.

    Judith: My father puttered in *his* garden nearly every evening after work. When he was a conscientious objector, in World War II, he gave over all his land to victory gardens, and all summer long the COs came to weed and hoe. Corn, in stiff straight lines, and cabbage, carrots, cauliflower—seemingly anything beginning with C. After we moved, my father delineated his garden with a stone wall, which he dismantled and then built again every time he decided to expand the garden. Since the garden had once, it seemed, been a streambed, he paid us by the bushel to pick up stones. Stones, he often claimed, were his best harvest. In back, by the cemetery fence, was a long row of raspberries and black caps. Then peas and beans and corn and squash—and cantaloupes, which he claimed had lost their taste now that he didn't have horse manure to start their seeds in. Just inside the wall, asparagus grew like wildfire. My mother was not a good cook, so the bounty was usually boiled past recognition, but she loved to bake and sometimes there would be a shortcake you could kill for, or a pie that melted in your mouth. Cherry, from the tree beside the garage, if the birds didn't get there first. And apple, if we could find some without worms (which my father claimed were 100 percent apple anyway, so we should simply close our eyes and bite).

7. Restaurants

Judith: Dinner was mostly for talk. And talk, for my father, meant loud discussion, bordering on fierce opinion and counteropinion in voices raised to a passionate pitch. So maybe, I'm thinking, the reason we never went to restaurants was because he would have had to force himself to do the kind of small, quiet talk he had no time for. In a restaurant, could he extol the virtues of Socialism, or rant about how the FBI had most certainly manufactured a typewriter to frame Alger Hiss? One year, we took a trip to New York City, where my father decided we should learn about Japanese food. Since he wouldn't ask directions, we walked several blocks east when we should have gone west, then had to turn around and redouble our efforts. I was so tired and hungry that I made him happy by trying the teriyaki, but my brother sat all through our meal, scowling, and then we had to find him a White Tower. That, come to think of it, could have been a deciding factor in our restaurantless life.

Fleda: My father's idea of dinner is eating. He eats as fast as possible and finds the occasion of sitting at the table not particularly comfortable for conversation. For that matter, he doesn't really like "conversation"—quiet talk, as you put it. Talk, for him, is for (1) transacting business, getting the green beans passed, and (2) arguing a point. If there is an argument to be had, splendid. But at dinner, it's hard to get worked up over tax policy and chew at the same time. It can be done, but it's more trouble to get up and find the book you're referring to, to prove your point. Furthermore, getting full is a top priority. Not waiting for your food is also a top priority. So it's easy to see that restaurants—where the act of eating is the experience—seem a waste to him. My father won't willingly go to a restaurant where you have to tip. Tipping makes him furious. Not because he thinks the wait staff doesn't deserve it, but because it's an added expense not on the price list, therefore ambiguous. Something about the unspoken obligation here sets him off. One time he and my mother were eating at Mrs. Pete's, a cheap local restaurant at the lake (dinner $4.95, dessert included), mother choked on a chicken bone. She would have died if Mrs. Pete hadn't done the Heimlich maneuver on her. After dinner, as usual, my father figured on a napkin the exact 10 percent tip, not a cent extra.

8. Arguments

Fleda: My father once said he didn't know why people talk except to convince someone or to learn something that might change their minds. For him, any exchange worth listening to is an exchange of information. He has several arguing points: 1) Einstein's theory of relativity has major flaws, and is basically wrong; 2) women don't like sex but pretend to, to get a man; 3) religion is the opiate of the masses; 4) the people responsible for tax policy in this country don't know what they're doing; 5) he himself is a worthless worm and incomparably stupid, but, surprisingly, there are people who appear to be stupider than he is.

In earlier days, the list would include issues of sailboat design. I have tried to argue with my father most of my life. I not only cannot win, I end up feeling stupid and helpless. I must not rely at any point on "I feel that," or "Well, what about their emotional welfare?" He doesn't think words themselves have any power. "If you call me an idiot and a liar, what's it to me? Those are only words," he says. And what's "emotional trauma"? What's religion, what's God? If you can't touch it, if you can't prove it, well—and here he gets his little-boy snide smile that says the foolishness at this point is beyond words.

Judith: My father was never so happy as when he could be organizing a movement against something. Somewhere under his curly red hair there was a place that never shut down. Ideas, inventions, ideologies, all simmering in the same soup. He had long before turned his back on any church, but he could conjure up a word-perfect King James to shore up any argument. He could march out science to pick apart anyone's carelessly constructed opinion. He was fearless in his use of stockpiled facts and his natural conversation was filled with "theorem," and "proof," and "therefore." Much as he liked the argument, however, he was uncomfortable with anything that had an emotional edge. For that matter, I realize now that he didn't know how to identify emotions, so they must have taken him by surprise almost every time. Little things like jealousy or depression or, really, even anger just blew right past him. Once, when my brother and I were having an argument, he decided to stand up on a chair and orchestrate it, waving his arms like a conductor at a symphony, allowing each of us a certain amount of time, asking for crescendo and diminuendo until we all burst out laughing.

9. Feminism

Judith: I would like to say my father was an early feminist. I was allowed to climb in the highest trees—trees I probably would not have allowed my sons to climb—and given baseball mitts and taught how to use a hammer. These gestures, I came to understand, were a form of love. He certainly never said the word. Nor did he cuddle or cherish. He had no time for girlish things, like cheerleading or boyfriends or hairdos, and he teased mercilessly when we got to the stage of caring about the Top Ten musical hits, calling Eddie Fisher "Freddie Fisher," to our extreme embarrassment. In fact, I now possess a letter from the time when I was about thirteen in which he tells his brother, "Judy is foolish as all hell," and, thinking back, I suspect there is no better way to say it. Yet I don't remember him once clearing his plate from the table. This does not make him a hypocrite—not quite—because I honestly don't think that he translated ideas to practicalities. I think this almost characterizes the times—those eccentric scientists, shored up by women who made it possible for them to keep the clouds over their heads. Certainly it was replicated in all my parents' friends. The word "couple" meant one who worked, one who helped the other be able to work. Housework, for all its second syllable, didn't count. Besides, anyone could see it was make work—why make a bed you're just going to be getting back into? He did take the initiative in anything that extended beyond the garage. He brought his physics into play more than once in cutting down trees, even huge mature maples. Usually he was fairly accurate about how to drive a wedge so that the tree wouldn't land in the middle of a forsythia bush, and he always told us the line to stand behind, but he often forgot about the way a tree will try to fool you with its own version of a recoil, and at least twice a tree rebounded to within an inch or two of the house.

Fleda: I think I grew up feral. My father didn't like imposing limits on anyone—that would have required an assumption that he knew better. Once I ordered from Sears an unfinished bookcase for my room, paid for it with my own slowly and hard-earned babysitting money. I took the bookcase to the backyard to varnish it. After I'd already made a mess of it, not sanding it first, blobbing up heavy coats of grass-infused varnish that ran down in rivulets, he mentioned, casually, that I might have put it on wooden blocks, and sanded first. How was I supposed to know? When I was learning to drive, he yelled that I was an idiot when I cut a corner too close and made the car in the intersection back up to let me by. He didn't tell me to swing out. He "assumed" that I could drive instead of teaching me how. As far as women in general went, my father had strong opinions. Women. They want, want, want things, and they're hopelessly illogical. His daughters got the message—if we were to count in the world, if we were not to be humiliated, we were to be like men. The measure of our success, however, rested solely on whether or not we could make a man happy.

10. Names

Fleda: My father's name is Phillips Hamlin Brown. His first name is his mother's maiden name. Mother always called him Phillips. Most people mishear and call him Phillip. Some jump right to Phil. He has no preference. This is an important issue, here—he doesn't think of himself as a Phil, or a Phillips. He doesn't think of himself. He is a lacuna among beings. He builds his existence out of argument, out of dissention, out of primal need. My mother's name was Mabel Frances Simpich. She didn't like Mabel. Her family called her "sister." She took on the nickname Tancy early in her marriage. She married my father when she was twenty, after two years in what was essentially a finishing school. She offered that information timidly, when she had to. She who spent most of her life as a housewife taking care of a brain-damaged son, who might she be, herself? She didn't know. She had rudimentary opinions about things, clichés about politics and religion. She wanted to please. She named me after both her mother-in-law and her mother—Fleda Sue. Her mother wanted me to have the two names legally fused together—Fledasue—so that her own name wouldn't be "lost" when I got married. All of which leads me into thinking about how a person's gradual taking of ownership of a name marks a passage into consciousness.

   Judith: I was supposed to be named after grandmothers as well—my father's grandmothers, Christina and Letitia. But there was some dissension over which was to be first, and I ended up with Judith, after no one, and without a middle name. My father's name was Bob.

His own father, who had been a professor, had gone by "Doctor" for so long even his wife sometimes referred to him that way. We didn't know it was strange to call our father by his first name.

When my children were little, they also naturally called him Bob. I didn't think too much about it until I heard one of them saying to a friend, "Where does your Bob live?" Where did our Bob live? I do not think he thought of himself as son, husband, father, though (with my mother's prodding) he dutifully played those roles. As a husband, he provided, and he seemed to enjoy the social life my mother assiduously provided in return. As a father, he liked to set us free. This was a conscious plan on his part, not happenstance. He refused to help with homework in any other form than asking us questions to lead us toward figuring things out for ourselves. He was never so happy as when he could be shaping our minds by refusing to shape them.

11. Books

Judith: Our house was full of books, though most of them looked rather dreary in their drab leather casings, and the magazines that arrived were stark in their black-and-white intellectualism. I envied my friends, whose parents subscribed to the *Saturday Evening Post* or even *Life*, with its photographs to alleviate the boredom. Socialism, I thought, must be synonymous with a kind of austere earnestness. But books were my way out into the world. Soon I realized that the author was the key to my particular pleasures. Once I found an author I enjoyed, I would read everything that person had written. So it was not surprising that in high school I was studiously devouring Hemingway, Fitzgerald, Steinbeck, then Faulkner. My father could not understand this. Why not wait until the critics decided which was the best book by any particular author, then read that one? This question marks the first sense I had that my father's wisdom was not infinite. And if he could be wrong about these things, he might not be right about larger things—like pacifism, or, for that matter, God. Well, in the end I granted him the lack of God, but only after I "rebelled" and went to church for one full year where, in Sunday school, I was told that if God did not want me to die, I could jump out the window right that minute and I would not fall to my death. What kind of God would defy his own law of gravity for a silly thirteen-year-old? Being my father's daughter, that was the quick demise of my willed belief.

Fleda: Alas, the books in my house amounted mostly to my father's economics textbooks, an old set of *Compton's Pictured Encyclopedia* from the days my father was selling them door-to-door, trying to earn enough money to get us through the summer, a few popular novels my mother checked out from the library, a thick book of Favorite Poems, and several dictionaries. Nothing was more important in my house than the dictionary. The house was saturated with words. My father started in on "T'was Brillig. . . . The road was a ribbon of moonlight. . . . O Captain my Captain. . . . The boy fell on the burning deck. . . ." and on and on, at the slightest inspiration. He was in a high school recitation group—he must know a hundred poems. On irregular Saturdays I climbed the narrow, steep stairs to the old library in Fayetteville, Arkansas, and checked out my limit. I had no guidance and mostly read beneath my ability. I liked to dash through easy books. As a teenager, I saturated myself in Ricky Nelson, Elvis, Tab Hunter, Pat Boone. I was aggressively determined to be "normal," and reckoned I had a lot to learn in that department. I was in my thirties before I noticed that my father never read fiction. Fiction is for women—the entire realm of the emotions is for women. He snidely dismisses all traits typically associated with the feminine. And the poems? Part of his attitude is Victorian, I'd guess, inherited from his father: literature as decoration around the edges of serious life, poems as lively interludes that tell a good story—like "The Song of Hiawatha" or "The Highwayman."

12. Stuck

Fleda: I have to say, now, that I'm worn out with this. I'm worn out with describing his foibles, his weirdnesses. I've spent much of my life listening to people chuckle tenderly—or belly laugh—at them, as if he were a sweet eccentric. Where can I go from here unless I go back into the dark, through the doors I don't want to open again, because the other rooms are there, too: the Other other, is the pain, the invisibility of a little girl desperate to please, a little girl who sees that if she isn't smart enough, if she acts like a girl, she'll be humiliated, crushed. A little girl who sees too much, who hears too much, who hides under the covers, who emerges with bravado, terrified inside. I am too old for this, for psychoanalyzing my father, my mother. I have lost interest, in the interest of my own aging. I've also maybe grown kind. We are dark and light, we are sometimes outside our own control. I have compartmentalized his life, holding each facet to the light, trading stories for a reaction from the group around the table, drinking wine. Literature as decoration, in the dim pub-light. All laughing. I get to be the star of the story, the teller. But now it's no longer a true story. It's me, telling a story. What was is dimmed and fogged. I know what is: a lonely old man who loves his daughters, a man who's become my child I half abandon, who my mind frequently abandons. I forget to call. I take on the guilt I've been given, the guilt of a first child who's pretty sure everything depends on her. A child who's failed to keep her parents safe from death, who's failed to keep them happy, who's failed to properly say who they are.

Judith: Even though we laugh, these men were powerful. Their very eccentricities made them more compelling in our eyes. Not like the fathers of my friends, who could be counted on to hug their daughters, or drive us to the movies. Who wore ironed shirts and had their hair cut at the barbershop? Who was this man who loomed so large? You're lucky you can think in present tense. Now there is only what was—and that will never be enough. I tell—and retell—the story of the last words he said to me. He was scheduled for a complicated surgery, and I was headed for my younger son's wedding. My brother stayed behind. Before I left, I told him on the phone I was so glad he was my father. I guess I imagined that under stress I might hear what I had never heard before. I'm still surprised at how surprised I was when he answered, "Well, I'll see you—remember O.J. was framed." That was 1995, halfway through the trial. I tell that story often. And I laugh. I even have some choice rejoinders. The past grows bright with what we might have said. In honor of his honesty, I'll say that I do not have his open goodness of the heart. But when I think of him, I don't feel guilt. This is all I have—this frame, this work of words. We were stuck with each other.

Past tense: Did we say all this that night? Not all of it. When it was fully dark and the wineglasses and beer mugs were empty, and the young woman came out, eager for us to finish up and leave, we wrapped our sweaters closer in the cool West Coast summer evening and headed back to our dorms, retelling bits and pieces to bring back the laughing part. Laughter's what we craved. The rest comes out, came out more slowly, later.

Native Bees

Native bees are mostly tiny and mostly don't sting. They are the neutrinos of the U.S.A., burrowing and threading everything together, fastening this to that with their dainty proboscis. But the country is beginning to wear thin; holes are showing up.

The furry half-inch-long "tickle bee," genus *Andrena*, lives in holes in the ground. It is the mascot of Sabin Elementary School in Portland, Oregon. It doesn't sting; it tickles. On warm days in Portland, when bees are flying in search of nectar, you can't walk across a field without bumping into dozens of them.

My mother loved to tickle. No matter my father's rants, her tears, my brother's seizures, she would for these brief interludes become a child, chasing us all over the house, finally getting us down on the bed and tickling us until we could hardly catch our breath for laughing. There was the tingling terror, the dash down the hallway, her pursuit, the laughter. These days tickling can be considered child abuse.

Chinese tickle torture is an ancient form of torture practiced in particular in the courts of the Han Dynasty. It was a punishment for nobility, since it left no marks and a victim could recover relatively easily and quickly. People who die of tickling usually die of cardiac arrest or asphyxiation.

Unlike the honeybee, a bumblebee's stinger lacks barbs, so the bee can sting repeatedly without injuring itself; the stinger is not left in the wound. Bumblebees are not normally aggressive, but may sting in defense of their nest, or if harmed.

"Tickle" is possibly a form of "tick" (v.) in its older sense of "to touch." A translation of Latin *titillare* in the late fourteenth century meant "to excite agreeably." Like "titillate."

Native bees are in steep decline.

Bumblebees were shipped from Europe to pollinate crops and brought a fungus that killed the wild bees. As with the Indians and small-pox, no one was aware what could happen if the natural barriers were broached.

I hated tickling. Tickling was the one thing she could do to get a belly laugh going. Sometimes I would try to pretend it didn't tickle. I didn't want to be helpless like her. I was already building a wall.

If we build a wall the Mexicans will pay for it, so says the president. No, they say. They won't. The Berlin Wall was built free and overnight by the East Berlin government with barbed wire, a death strip, and guard towers. Border length around West Berlin was

96 miles. Wall height was 11.8 feet. 66 miles of concrete, 41.3 miles of barbed wire.

The areas of the brain that are responsible for the tickle sensation are the primary somatosensory cortex and secondary somatosensory cortex. It has also been found that these areas of the brain are activated upon an anticipated tickle. Scientists feel that this is a response mechanism that we developed to protect ourselves against danger.

A columnist went incognito to a Donald Trump rally. He described the audience as mostly older white men who were literally trembling with anger, shaking their fists, shouting invectives. They were ready. They anticipated a violation of their native space. They were ready to cause violation, if need be, to stop it from happening.

According to psychologists: the husband, say, does his best to force his wife to leave him because he is so afraid she'll leave him. He pushes her to the edge of collapse, so if she stays, she must love him.

Colony Collapse Disorder (CCD) occurs when the majority of worker bees in a colony disappear and leave behind a queen, plenty of food, and a few nurse bees to care for the remaining immature bees. Either the workers sense impending danger and leave, or they've already been demolished by it.

When I left home and got married so young, was I running to or from? A case could be made for either. She couldn't leave my father. She had to stay put and take care of my brother, and besides, where would she go, what would she do? And who's to say what would have been best? She had her happinesses. Her Coke and ice cream. After my brother died, she took care of babies in the hospital nursery, a real job she loved, one she understood.

To build a bee house, take lumber scraps to make a box. Drill 5/16-inch holes, but not all the way through the wood. Cover the holes with chicken wire to keep birds away. Keep the bee house on the south side of a building and do not move it until at least November. Do not spray insecticides.

Rachel Carson in the fifties began writing about the devastation of insects from insecticides, which was met with fierce opposition by chemical companies.

You can be out of control with laughing, even if you have a deep sadness that is like the flu. The sadness may be personal, but it may be the deep sadness of the country. Echinacea is of the aster family, is a favorite of bees, and combats colds and flu in humans. It was used by Native Americans long before the Europeans settled. It became much more popular after the Germans did research on it in the 1920s.

My mother loved laughing the most. She was not ticklish, so she could be The Tickler. She said she wasn't ticklish. I kept trying, but really she wasn't.

The fuzzy-legged leafcutter bee uses its furry front legs to cover the eyes of females during mating, probably to stop the females being distracted by other males during copulation. Qualities that seem unusual have an evolutionary survival advantage.

*   *   *

People known to be ticklish tense up when another goes to tickle them, making them easy to tickle. You can learn to be not ticklish by relaxing your muscles and "giving permission" to be tickled and stay relaxed. You could imagine you are in a different country with no tickling. But this doesn't explain why some people are more sensitive in the first place.

If you got stung by a lot of bees, you might die, but also bee venom is given as a shot for rheumatoid arthritis, nerve pain, and multiple sclerosis, which apparently causes the immune system to become desensitized. The effort to heal oneself can go amuck. My mother had gold salts for her arthritis, and then steroids later. When the body has been working so hard to defend itself, it produces inflammation, which can be reduced by both methods.

Laughter, no matter how artificial, improves your immune system and relieves pain. There should have been more laughter.

The honeybee's hysterical waggle dance, performed inside the hive by forager bees, tells their hive mates about a food source. Directional information may be established by gravity, but there is evidence that it has to do with the magnetic field.

There should be more laughter.

The direction is toward survival. Gravity pulls inward toward the greatest mass, what might be crumpled on a bed, crying, or rioting outside the places of power. Magnetism is made up of small charged particles flying around like bees regulated only by a north-south polarity.

Everyone has a tickle spot. My mother knew exactly where to get me. I admit I was furious and laughing at the same time. I was glad for the laughter.

My sister posted a photo of a bumblebee on a blossom of her Meyer lemon tree in Texas. She said she had trouble getting the bee to hold still. She's very funny. The tree is generously holding still to allow the bee to tickle its lily-like blossoms. The tree is aware in its flowing and hardening bark that it has to do its part to save the entire country.

Strong Brown God

The Mississippi River touches me. I get this kind of hopeful-hopeless feeling, like Huck Finn, who saw the damned human race pretty much accurately, but had a good time anyway. Twain said the river "will always have its own way; no engineering skill can persuade it to do otherwise." This "sullen" and "intractable" river, as T. S. Eliot called it—something about its basic and necessary flooding and sandbars and flat farmland—leaves me without imaginative resources. What can I make of it?

Eliot called it a "strong brown god." The name "Mississippi" comes from the Anishinaabe people. It means something like "Big River" or "Father of Waters." I have its messy meandering mixed up with my father. My family moved to Missouri, beside the river, when I was in high school and my father, these fifty-two years later, still lives there. It is not my native land, but it goes on pulling along its soil, cutting through the heart of the country whether I claim it or not.

My father is ninety-five. By the time you read this he may be dead, but no matter: like the river he'll keep going on in me. I'm leaning one way, he's leaning another, and together we'll arrive at the Gulf, all spread out and unrecognizable. That's Swinburne: "Even the loneliest river / winds somewhere safe to sea."

He lives in a retirement community, now, in an independent living cottage. He wanted to move there because Lois, his lady friend of over fifteen years, is in assisted living there. So he's always eaten meals with that group, pointedly ignoring the benefits of eating with and joining the activities of the independent living crowd. He has some degree of Asperger's, never diagnosed, not labeled by us, his daughters, until a few years ago. Oh. Yes. That's it. A found name. Like Desoto "found" the Mississippi River. It was never "lost," naturally. It's been there since the glaciers melted. But no sooner than we found Asperger's, the DSM took it away again. Now there's only the "autism spectrum." He's probably low on the spectrum.

The old people are at the table long before dinner is served, waiting. Eerily, there's no fidgeting, no restlessness. Waiting is one of the important items to be ticked off in the day, part of the ritual of eating. There's little talk, a few words here and there, almost nothing that could pass for conversation. Several residents have trouble holding up their heads. They loll forward in wheelchairs, sometimes almost to the table. Then there is my father, holding forth with his mouth full, about economics (he has an MBA from Harvard and an all-but-dissertation PhD from the University of Missouri), politics, religion, clock mechanisms, or motors, in his penetrating voice to anyone who'll nod in his direction, who'll acknowledge his words enough to give him impetus to go on. He has dutifully put his napkin in his lap, although he never uses it.

He's quite handsome, still, even with a gap showing where a couple of teeth are missing (he thinks he's too old now to spend the money for new ones). He's tall but stooped, with a full head of steely gray hair, slicked straight back. His dirty glasses are held together on one side with Scotch tape. His pants, stained, belted high and far too short, are from Goodwill, two dollars a pair. Most days he wears his cast-off UPS jacket. The soles of his old brown shoes are worn smooth. But considering the competition, he's a Greek god.

A weird one. It's a relief to have some name, any name, for what had always been his maddening eccentricity, his inability to recognize or respond accurately to feelings. The reason he's stuck with assisted living is that he's never had what you would call friends. He latches on to a woman. His sex life with her constitutes his emotional life. I get that now—feelings need to be tangible for him to recognize them. Touch. Fondling. Kissing. Yuck. This is my father I'm talking about.

There's always been that degree of yuck, since he never fails to articulate everything that passes through his head. There are no filters. So we've always known every detail of his sex and digestive life. When mother was alive, she kept him reined it, to some extent, but now he tells us everything he can manage before we ask him to shut up.

So here's the situation. My husband Jerry and I arrive to visit him. He opens the door and gives us quick pat-hugs before he turns back to the guts of an ancient VCR player spread out on the floor. He's found what appears to be the culprit, a small fuse that "is worth about 20 cents that I'll have to pay $2.50 for," he says. But it might not be the culprit. There appears to be a chipped place on a plastic part.

He could use the VCR on his TV, but the tapes he uses are so old—he won't buy new ones—that they're wrinkled and often get stuck. With a separate machine, he can take the top off and disentangle the tape.

He's on the floor, grunting and wheezing over the broken machine. Then it's a quarter to five, time to go to dinner. Jerry and I don't plan to eat there—the food is white, bland, and overcooked—but we sit with him while he eats. We tell him we're just not hungry yet. The old people are almost all seated when we come in. We hug Lois, who is so glad to see us she almost cries. She's quite demented but has no trouble knowing who we are, even asking about the family. She used to come to Michigan with my father, staying a good portion of every summer. They have been like a married couple for many years. Now she's in a wheelchair and spends most of her day in bed, using oxygen off and on.

That is the problem. Her family has said she can't walk over to my father's cottage anymore. She might fall. Long before, they forbade her to ride to the senior center with him for lunch—the one place he continues to drive.

I am thinking of the look of sheer panic on my father's face when I left after mother's funeral. I would say it might be recognition of loss, of sadness. Or of fear of not being able to take care of himself. Those would be reasonable feelings. But I knew. It was the loss of sex. I bolstered his morale by telling him the casserole ladies would be beating a path to his door. He smiled a wan smile. Sure enough, within two months he had a new lady, Lois.

Lois became part of our lives. "She's not very smart," our father said, "and definitely not pretty," but she seemed to love him and was willing to ramp up her sex life again, long after her husband died, and she thought she was "done with all that." She's a sweet lady. She grew her white hair long to please him. She used to bake heaps of cookies when we were all at the cottage. She enjoyed our children and grandchildren. Her own daughter is something of a martinet, and her family seemed to be barely willing to put up with her. They were resentful of my father, always. I can't really blame them much for that. He's not your average prince charming.

Lois doesn't know about Phyllis. This is what my father claims. But when we visited Lois's room, I saw that from her one window, the one she can't help but look out of when she's lying in bed, she has a perfect view of the porch and front door of my father's cottage. Which is where Phyllis can be found every evening after he leaves Lois.

He's faithful to Lois, in his fashion. He has dinner at her table every night and goes to her room afterward to sit and hold her hand and watch TV with her for a couple of hours. It's their time together. Then he leaves her and meets Phyllis at his place. They go to bed together.

I won't describe all I know here. As I said, my father has managed, against my wishes, to let me in on the details of his sex life. I won't perpetuate that, and you don't want to know, anyway. Likewise, I could describe his chronic constipation and the exact measures he takes to combat it. I could describe his bowel movements.

Morgan runs the facility where this intrigue is taking place. I visit her alone, to check on things with my father. "Lois had a hard time with his relationship with Phyllis at first," she says. "Lois saw them kissing." Oh. Oh, no. Lois knew from the start. I am slightly sick. I am furious. Poor Lois.

My fury is nothing new. I could give you history. What if everything I write, everything I've written, is driven by wrath at my father? What if my poems are secret codes to slip by his incessant lecturing? He's the river running through my life; I'm building sea walls, dykes. That would be a nice metaphor. Or, you might say I'm trying to figure out what any of this means. Or you could say I'm shaping the truth the way I want. I am not so sure of anything. What if the sum total of writing, of art, is just the same downhill movement as the river, just sliding toward the sea, carrying what it picks up along the way? No special reason. Just because this is how things are. People write. People behave in sane and insane ways. What they do has so many different causes it's useless to try to find one, or two.

Actually, the river is an ideal image for my father. It goes on and on, carrying its cargo of silt and barges, oblivious to any damage it causes. I'm now sixty-eight. I have never persuaded my father of anything. Neither has anyone else. Case in point: his letters on the subject of religion. Pages and pages, typed on his manual typewriter, single spaced. He is in perfect agreement with Twain's heretical *Letters from the Earth*. He listens to Hal Holbrook reading from it whenever he wants to cheer himself up. Here's a small bit on how heaven came into being that makes my father hoot with joy: "In time, the Deity perceived that death was a mistake; a mistake, in that it was insufficient . . . it allowed the dead person himself to escape from all further persecution in the blessed refuge of the grave. This was not satisfactory. A way must be conceived to pursue the dead beyond the tomb."

My father is afraid of dying. Well, he's afraid of the act of dying, not of being dead. He is tired of living and wants to get the dying part over with. "Where is Jack Kevorkian when you need him?" he frequently says. He's willed his body to the University of Missouri medical school, for studying. I would say I've already studied him sufficiently, but maybe there will be something left for them.

Meanwhile, at least there's Phyllis. She is at least in her seventies and has never had a man in her life before. He tells us she says her relationship with my father is the best thing that's ever happened to her. My father had described her to us like this: "She has a couple of teeth missing in front and is kind of pudgy, but she loves me desperately."

His description proved to be pretty accurate. She used to be a math teacher but is now somewhat demented, although less so than Lois. Her family put her here and have threatened to move her somewhere else. They came to visit one evening and she wasn't in her room. They found her at my father's, both of them "undressed," as Morgan carefully described it.

Morgan talked to Phyllis's guardians. She reminded them that Phyllis is happy, and that if they move her, she'll be lonely and will probably search out another companion. She's not being harmed, she assured them. But, still, there's the looming possibility that one day she won't be there.

We take my father for a drive to Cape Rock Park one day—territory where he used to ride his bike and hike the trails. We call Morgan and ask if Lois can go, but she says Lois is too weak and her family doesn't want her to leave the facility. I know the truth—they don't want her to go anywhere with my father.

He has his routine carefully orchestrated. We spend requisite time in Lois's cluttered little room. Jerry and I have brought her a mug from Michigan, a touristy kind of thing she raves over and probably forgets ten minutes later. Or maybe not. Dementia is mysterious. Just when it seems all is forgotten, the mind turns lucid again. There's nothing to do but hope that our kindness is remembered, at least in bits and pieces, at least in a feeling, if not remembered facts.

Then we leave. I ask my father the next day if Phyllis came over when we left. "Oh, yes," he says, smiling sheepishly.

"Do you know that Lois can look directly from her window and see your front door?" I ask him. "She can see every time Phyllis comes over."

"Oh, well, if she looks," he replies. As if this would be an almost impossible rarity.

"She can't help but look," I say. "She'd have to be blind not to see." He doesn't seem to hear.

I try to imagine how he's thinking about all this. What I figure is that he is almost completely unaware of the emotional life around him, so he can't imagine that Lois would see, either. This theory at least keeps me from the urge to summon Kevorkian back from the grave. And maybe Lois is too far gone to remember for more than a few minutes what she sees. All this is about tone, and feeling, though, what floats unseen, what can't be assembled or reassembled.

The next morning, my father is trying to get the cover back on the VCR. He's giving up, for now. I wash up a few plates but give up quickly. Let him live his own life. There's a knock on the door. It's Phyllis. We've been introduced to her formally, in the midst of other people, but this is the first time we've been introduced to her as my father's woman. She seems just as he pictured her, silky, thinning white hair to her shoulders, pudgy, a few teeth missing. I think maybe she is less gentle, a bit tougher than Lois.

"I want to demonstrate something," he tells us. He carefully positions himself directly in front of Phyllis, legs slightly apart for balance, and reaches for her. He kisses her passionately. "I love her and she loves me," he says. "Thank you," she says.

"Well, good," is all I can think of to say. He's like a child showing us his new toy. I am seeing the line of succession, the women he's intended to love and has, in his way, starting with my mother. He's carried on along the course of his life, slamming into the banks, dragging along logs, carving out new channels at the expense of whatever's in the way. Not unkind, always meaning the best, really. But oblivious.

After lunch we take him to Trail of Tears State Park. It's good to have something to do, a goal, something else to focus on. Meandering through the park roads, we accidentally find the overlook. My father remembers having been here many times. He's excited. We walk out to the end, among a group of motorcyclists who have stopped, also. My father walks flat-footed, like a slightly drunk man, on his weak legs, but he's glad to be here after so many years. You can see miles of the river and what seems like an island on the other side. You can see the tiny sticks of a cross on a distant mountain. Someone lends my father binoculars, which he can't get adjusted.

In Twain's day, it was both better and worse. People dumped all sorts of things in it—dead gamblers, empty gin bottles, barrels, sewage, rotten dog carcasses, felled trees. As long as the riverboats and barges could get through, no one much complained. I remember my father saying years ago that if you swam in the Mississippi, you probably wouldn't die *right away*.

Yet in the back of our collective minds, there's Huck and Jim on that raft:

> We slid into the river and had a swim, so as to freshen up and cool off; then we set down on the sandy bottom where the water was about knee deep, and watched the daylight come. Not a sound, anywhere—perfectly still . . . sometimes the bull-frogs a-cluttering . . . then a pale place in the sky; then more paleness, spreading around, then the river softened up . . . you could see a streak on the water which you know by the look of the streak that there's a snag there in the swift current which breaks on it . . . and you see the mist curl up off the water, and the east reddens up.

Thick and deep through the heart of this country runs the "getting away from everything" romance, the "light out for the territory" story that critics and philosophers delight in applying to everything American.

My father always wanted to get away, to sail around the world. He designed and built five sailboats. He'd be alone. Or with a woman; that would be better. He spent a good part of my childhood trying to design a self-steering mechanism. He'd be out there, opening his can of beans, reading, and managing the wind. You can know the wind, even if it shifts. You can see how far to head into it, you can calculate how much sail to let out or bring in. With humans, well, they're a puzzlement. When his mind turns to their foibles and their political stupidities, he is mostly just plain astonished. Like Huck and Jim, floating along, coming ashore at night, dealing briefly with the baffling human race, then returning to the river.

After Trail of Tears, we take my father to Olive Garden to eat. We're going home tomorrow. He has a fainting spell as soon as we sit down.

Oh, dear, too much activity, too much noise and confusion. He recovers enough to eat a salad, but we should have known better. He needs his routine. We take him home. He sits in the chair this time, fooling hopelessly with the VCR, pulling the cover off again, wiggling various parts. He leans back slowly, turning pale, and we realize he's having another fainting spell—quickly over with, but still.

I go over to the main office and find a nurse. Since my father's in independent living, he's not supposed to be eligible for medical care, but she comes over and takes his vitals. Blood pressure okay, a little high, pulse high, a little low on the oxygen saturation. She thinks he should move to assisted living. Probably everyone thinks he should.

What does life feel like when there's no place left to go, no "territory" to head out into, when your world comes down to one room with a few memorabilia, which you are oblivious to? Who has considered what happens at that time when others turn to an inner life, but you can't find one? You have only your facts, your tangible things.

I am not going to move my father yet. How could he be "saved" with closer watching? He has his women. His broken VCR. We get a letter from him almost as soon as we get home. He writes that he'll be dead in six months, he's pretty sure. I wouldn't be surprised. He usually knows what he's talking about. I hope he dies in his sleep, after a nice evening kissing Phyllis. Touching someone, being touched, to remind himself that he exists.

Inside the Conch Shell

"Originality," Jane Hirschfield reminds me, "requires the aptitude for exile." I sure enough have the aptitude, yet here I am, on my way to visit my father. It takes me six, maybe eight minutes to walk from our large brick condo building at Grand Traverse Commons down the path, over the little wooden bridge, and across the lawn to his place at Willow Cottage Assisted Living. We moved him from Missouri to Michigan a year ago, in May. He calls me or I call him, or visit him, almost every day.

When I left home, basically I wanted the hell out of there, physically and psychologically—away from my brain-damaged brother and his constant seizures, from my whole family, but mostly from my father. Now look.

✳   ✳   ✳

"When are you going to quit writing about your family?" This was Gerald Stern. He'd just picked my second book of poems as winner of a contest, and he'd stopped in Delaware on his way home to New Jersey to help me with revision. As I drove him back to the train station, that's what he said.

That was twenty years ago. Haven't I grown up yet? Haven't I had enough of this? This rehashing, this perpetual dusk of childhood. I'm tired of it; really I am. Haven't I exhausted the subject?

I submit to you James Baldwin, who insists that "the responsibility of a writer is to excavate the experience of the people who produced him." Excavate. Not your own experience, but that of those who produced you. What produced William Blake? Heaven is his mother, Hell his father, or vice versa. What produced Emily Dickinson? She can hardly bear to look. Donald Hall, when asked what he writes about, blurted out, "Love, death, and New Hampshire." It seems as if a core requirement for this work is an obsession with solving the great mystery of our existence by filling in enough background with our words so that we become visible. Even our fictions, maybe especially our fictions, are filling in what might have been there—what *is* there in the alternate world that's able to illuminate this one.

Rilke writes to the young writer Baladine Klossowska that "in order for a Thing to speak to you, you must regard it for a certain time as *the only one that exists*, as the one and only phenomenon which, through your laborious and exclusive love, is now placed at the center of the universe."

So there he is, my father, his stentorian voice cutting through all attempt at conversation. Day after day he passionately struggles with his books, with his mind, to prove Einstein wrong. All my life. Not for any reason except the rule of reason, which my father supposedly maintains. He was an economist, about as close as you can get to a full-blooded scientist without being one.

Already I am falling back into the pit here, attempting to explain him to you again, all the way to the bottom. There is no bottom. The blackness down there is my confusion. Why am I confused? I know how he is—a person with functional autism, full of old poems and dates and names and other things I am not full of. I cannot recite my own poems; he can recite all of Alfred Noyes's "The Highwayman," plus dozens of others. He's ninety-eight.

Within a couple of months of my father's arrival, he was on the printed weekly activities program at Willow—Wednesdays, he reads poems to the other residents. He loves this, spending hours picking through the books we've brought him plus his God-knows-how-old *101 Favorite Poems*. He wheels up to the third floor, where tea and cake are being served, skips the tea and cake because he was told he was spilling it all over himself trying to read at the same time. He doesn't notice such things. His clothes get filthy in one day.

*   *   *

What can be done? My mother cried and folded clothes. Isn't the creative life about folding clothes while crying? Organizing through it all—not *because of* but *through*. Our gesture. Yet the subject has spoken to me so loudly that all my experience compacts subtly inside its shape. I resent his crowding out. I have resented it all my life. Crowd out my mother, crowd out my sisters, crowd out me. You could call my poems small hidden rebellions. He might be in them, but he can't figure them out. They aren't rational. Longfellow is rational. Robert Service. Poe. Tennyson. At least by my father's lights. It isn't that he refuses to see beyond. He *cannot* see beyond. So I let my attention merge, meander, emerge, locate itself both here and in the beyond where he can't pester me.

*   *   *

He wanted to read two of my poems to the group. He's puzzled, can't get why something's a poem that doesn't rhyme and doesn't have a clear story. In some way he's proud of me, but not sure whether what I do merits it. I have all these books but that makes no sense to him. I'd rather he didn't read my poems, I think. Well, I'm pleased, but. . . . This is what I mean by wanting to locate myself where his rationality can't hurt me. He won't make fun of my work, but he won't like it. I'm surprised by how much this matters to me.

Yet I need you to see how interesting he is, with his one leg, wheeling around his tiny assisted-living room after another book! Or fixing his three clocks, one of which he has turned on its side to make it keep the right time. This is the wind-up clock, the one we bought him because he said he wanted an alarm clock.

He wanted an alarm clock because his days are full, so he'd better get at it. The young women come to help him walk with his prosthesis. He will never master this. He is ninety-eight—I told you that. He can walk a short way down the hall with a walker, but that's all. The attention is what he wants. And the challenge. In his eighties, he won three hundred-mile medals from his bike club. He was their patron saint. But, as did everything else, that activity fell away with no regrets, no looking back. Now it's this.

*   *   *

Does he even think about my mother? He's settled into his story that he didn't mean to marry her. He just asked in a letter (he was in the army, in the Philippines at the time) what she would say *if* he asked her to marry him, and, he says, the next thing he knew, she sent him the engagement notice from the newspaper. Maybe, maybe not. I dug through the heaps of photos and papers when we cleaned out the house. I found both the engagement announcement and, among his letters, a poem he wrote her while he was overseas. It's full of poetic cliché and forced rhyme, but if he wasn't in love with my mother, he was certainly in love with love, and with language. Here's an excerpt:

> *The fog is closing in. I sit alone*
> *And watch the blinking lights across the bay*
> *Or 'neath the haloed moon with its soft play*
> *Of silver light upon the pebbled strand*
> *I hear the tinkling wavelets on the sand. . . .*
> *Yet as I sit and gaze upon the scene*
> *So unsurpassed in beauty and serene*
> *As peace itself, within my breast*
> *There is a quiet but deep unrest,*
> *A secret longing not akin to pain,*
> *A yearning to come back to you again. . . .*

Now, in his room, we look at old photos. There's one he'd taken of another young woman back then. He says, "I would've married her [the other one] in a minute but I didn't think I could support a family." My mother was beautiful, I have to say. She tried all her life to please him. At least that's how it looked to me, but she grew to hate him, too, because he couldn't, just couldn't, have any real, normal feelings toward her. His attitude was clinical. She might have been anyone, was how it seemed. Any woman who isn't mean is as good as any other, he'd intimate frequently, although it's highly preferable to have an attractive one.

Flannery O'Conner says, "At its best our age is an age of searchers and discoverers, and at its worst, an age that has domesticated despair and learned to live with it happily." I was watching. I was entranced by the tangle. I thought the—yes, maybe happy—purpose of my life was to try to sort things out. Not to fix them, which I deemed impossible, but to understand. Her tears were easy to understand. But him? Entrancingly funny, as handsome as they come, remarkably skilled mechanically, and smart. Yet stupid, unable to see, strangely unaware of his own self, and unable to think abstractly at all (unless we're talking about physics, and, even then, on a mechanical level). Through the years, he has remained determined to get to the root of the time-space problem and to demonstrate that Einstein is simply nuts, literally and theoretically, to claim that person can travel into space and come back younger.

Here I am again, telling you a story. The "ferocious appetite" of sequential structure, as Ellen Bryant Voigt calls it, that keeps eating itself up, playing against the presumption of its stability. The lyric, on the other hand, Voigt calls "perception." Stopping, holding still. The points on a graph. Connect them and you have the narrative. There I was, a child, suffering because I was invisible, and because the world was scary, holding myself still and safe inside my thoughts. Look at me, all serious, thinking of God, of trees, making little forts in the woods. Making tiny bowls out of acorns. Staying small, thinking myself into smallness.

What is the relationship between seeing and feeling? We write words and they box us in. At the same time, they're our only tool to point toward the lump in the throat, the deep interior wound we call "parent."

∗　　∗　　∗

When I visit, he is working on time-space again. I sit, at the age of seventy-one myself, in the one chair in his room. I could be ten, or twenty, or any age. I am a fixture he can talk at.

Not that he doesn't value me. "I sure hope your cancer doesn't come back," he says frequently—his sledgehammer way of saying he cares. I know he worries that if I die, his finances might not be so well taken care of, but that's not fair of me to say, because I know he loves me as he can. Hard to sort these things out. Hard to remember what's now and what I've lugged along from the past.

Pills plus extreme old age have rendered him very sweet. There is a moment when neither of us can think what to say next. He smiles at me. This feels wonderful and terrifying, the lens scrubbed clean; here it is, I'm thinking, what was pushed away, driven away, covered over with fierce anger. The love, the hurt, the anguish. Me, looking into my own eyes. Me, writing to me.

∗　　∗　　∗

No wonder I resist writing these words. I am over my head. But what other words are there? What is the reason for writing anything? To *amuse, inspire, inform*—I learned that once. There is a reader out there: a *you*. "See," I say, "*you* have to see. He is too interesting to pass up."

When I was a child, I kept one eye always on the familial weather-vane. Will he see that Mother spent money on Kleenex brand instead of generic and take off on a rant? Will this simple rift in the fabric unleash the furies? Or will he start whistling in the garden and make all the angels sing? There is this unique being, this unique moment in time. They are on the move. I am born to trace their trajectory. My tracings will save my soul. And if I can bring you along, maybe I can shine a small light into our mutual great dark.

∗　　∗　　∗

He was living in Missouri when we got the call that he'd been taken to the hospital with leg pain. By the time my sister and I got there, the aneurysm behind his knee had been unsuccessfully repaired. The surgeon wanted to amputate his leg right away. But then the second surgeon said, when pressed, "I don't know. Maybe I wouldn't. Maybe he's better off just dying. The leg is beginning to rot; he'll go into a coma. Maybe letting him go is better than trying to put him through another surgery which could likely kill him anyway."

I kind of agreed with the second surgeon. My father was weak and tired, he'd said over and over that he didn't want to live any longer, and he hurt a lot. I laid out the blunt choices for him, but I was pretty sure what he'd say: I knew my father doesn't want to die. I suppose it would take a pretty strong or hopeless or depressed person to say *Yes, okay, I'll die now.* He said, of course, "Let's amputate."

Another surgeon was called in to do the operation, after hours on a Saturday evening. My sister and I did yoga stretches in the waiting room, expecting the worst. The surgeon came out. "Strong as an ox," he said. "His heart is fine. He'll be fine." And on rounds the next morning he asked, "How are you this morning, Mr. Brown?"

"Well, one leg's shorter than the other," said my father with a bemused smile.

✳   ✳   ✳

I am mourning the gap, the loss of his leg—well, all my losses—but my father is living in the present. My mind begins pouring its stored images and feelings into the gap. Sensations act as if they were still in the leg. Blank space refuses to remain blank. One thing follows another; before long, a string of thoughts and feelings coheres into a narrative. The horses' heads are turned toward eternity, Emily Dickinson surmised; we just start in and we go.

I did not want to get caught up in the narrative because that's not where my heart lies. My heart is a rip current, moving away from shore, cutting through the lines of breaking waves—a countervalent language, a language weaving shakily on one leg. I want somehow to leave Point A and get someplace that isn't Point B, but it's so hard, so much against. So uncertain is the goal, so uncertain the gait, that the traveling itself becomes the point.

*   *   *

His prosthesis works like this: most of the time he wears a stump-shrinker, a tight, stretchy item with a hard rubber base designed to fit into the prosthesis. Air bubbles can get between the skin and the stump-shrinker. You have to work those out. Then you need to pull on a specially designed heavy cotton sock to further pad the stump when you slide it into the hard plastic upper part of the prosthesis. Everything must be lined up so that the foot part will point straight ahead. The knee is a spring. The lower leg is a shining metal tube. The foot is foot-shaped metal and is wearing his new black tennis shoes. Shoe.

My father gets down the short hallway and has to take a break. The aide pushes his wheelchair behind him so he can sit. He works hard at this. Language works hard lugging the image across the perceived gap between then and now, and between the feeling of this and the way it appears.

*   *   *

Another thing: with only one leg to support himself, my father can't get his pants down fast enough to use the toilet, so he has to get out of his wheelchair, lie in bed, and use the urinal. He spills pee. His room smells. That information you could do without, but I am a kid walking into a room, saying, "Phew, it smells in here!" Wanting everyone to know. Wanting to stop the adult conversation cold and pay attention to what everyone's ignoring. Wanting a line break. Poised there for a half-second—as the pause Denise Levertov assigns to the end of a line of poetry—letting it rest on its own, without giving it value yet. Why did I tell you about the sadness of my mother? Happiness/sadness: same plot. The tide comes in, goes out, keeps us busy while the rip current cuts across, dangerously.

∗   ∗   ∗

I wheel him up to the third floor, where there is cake and tea. The residents are gathered around the table. He opens his *101 Poems* with its pink stickers to mark the pages. I sit across from him on the piano bench, where he can see me but I'm not interfering. He asks if he can read a little prose first. The audience isn't capable of much response: smiles and occasional clapping gestures—except for Bill, who smiles at almost everything. He likes my father. And there's frizzy-haired Nancy, who sits next to my father, pats him on the hand, and seems proud to sit there. He reads a passage from "My Last Walk with the Schoolmistress," by Oliver Wendell Holmes, a sentimental piece about the moment the speaker realizes he has his heart's desire, the love of the schoolmistress. They will never part again.

Here is what's baffling. My father is moved by this. And he is moved by a painfully sentimental poem called "My Mother's Hands." This is a man who says people love other people primarily because they want or need things. We do what we do because of our genetic predisposition. There is no free will. Love is explained by our desire to reproduce so that our genes will survive. Here I am on the piano bench, watching his chin tremble.

Who am I? Who is this person who left home, who made a life unrelated to her father, who thought of home as a place not to be from? I know nothing. Growing up I did not know who he was, and I do not now know. He reads the poem and the words take him under some surface. What lives there he knows not, but his chin is trembling. He is as mysterious as my own mind. He *is* my mind, what I made up. I was not wrong, I was not right.

It's a mess. Leads and tangles. You follow until the trail goes cold. You do this over and over. When there are no more leads, you stand there, hands at your sides, and watch the sunset. What accumulates when there is no clear point is *wonder*. The trembling, the rhythms of the substructure begin to be felt. Meaning does not accumulate in the retelling: awe does.

✳   ✳   ✳

I want language to mirror what I think is out there. What *seems* to be there. Yet what's there but what I've created? My words themselves create a solitude, a rounding down of my mind as if I'm in a conch shell. I start at the outer edge and curve inward until I can't see any farther. Father. I can't see any father. There is killing in the streets, there is war, there is ISIS, there is betrayal, there is child abuse. Not out there—not *just* out there. They're deep in here. When I keep looking, there's a point where they eventually must touch each other. Where they must be seen and touched with silence. With the countervalent force of silence.

✳   ✳   ✳

He goes on about the speed of light. Supposedly, the speed of light in a vacuum is the same no matter what. How can that hold equally true, he asks, if you're moving toward it or away from it? He says *red shift*, he says *Doppler effect*, he says *flashlights*, he says *stars*. The light of stars is the only thing we can see, not stars themselves. Unless they're close, like our sun. Then they're the real deal.

What is the real deal made of but light? Waves of electromagnetic radiation that arrive bundled into little packets called photons. Just energy in lumps, everything we see. These bundles of letters called words, these bundles of words called meaning. These bundles of metaphor, all of them, curling down inside themselves, hard little shells to contain the vastness, to hold off the vastness.

✳   ✳   ✳

Didn't I want to write poems because of their solitariness? Because of their curling, because their meaning reflects like nacre on the inside of a shell. Like a mirror. A classic Zen poem, "Song of the Jewel Mirror Samadhi," says:

The meaning is not in the words,
yet it responds to the inquiring impulse.
Move and you are trapped;
miss and you fall into doubt and vacillation.

My stories are held in suspension by the silence. To tell them, I have to press them against the membrane of words. I have to wrap my father in his scarf, his heavy coat, his knit cap, and push his wheelchair over to our place. The one leg rest catches on the concrete, so I take it off to raise it a bit. I can't. I can't get the metal nub to slide up to the next hole. "Let me see if I can do it," he says, and fixes it. So simple when you see the exact motion necessary.

✳   ✳   ✳

I wanted to get his attention. I wanted him to be proud of me. His attention has been on Einstein. Inside Einstein is a kingdom where people come back younger than when they left. Maybe they could live their lives again, try all this some other way. But if time and space are inseparable, if there is only space-time, there is no "some other way" and no "again." I have to get it right this time.

But what is "right"? Even Galileo figured out there is no absolute state of rest, no privileged reference frame. Things are in motion, and they are impenetrable, not to be figured out. There is only the play of stories—sorties and retreats.

Once upon a time there was my father. The word "once," that creates time: "time," that busily concocts a narrative. There was "father": that perception of separation, that gap between him and my understanding, between him and my need for love, for recognition. When my poem turned the corner at the end of the line, there was a satisfying feeling of being held back, held in; and also the grief of not being let in on a secret. But, still, the poem was an oxygen mask that allowed for breathing, when otherwise . . .

✳   ✳   ✳

The day looks promising for sailing, a good wind. My father is a skillful sailor and finds the gusts to travel on. Our lake is gusty. When we are beyond seeing, down by Recreation Point, the wind dies. I am twelve, seeing a little beyond my childhood but still ruled by it. We will not hear the dinner bell. They can't see us from around the point. He catches every slight breeze; we take turns with the one canoe paddle. I am full of despair and single-mindedness. I am full of joy.

Nothing has changed in the six intervening decades. I am in constant despair, constant joy. The connection called family is almost broken, but of course not really. "There is one story and one story only," Robert Graves wrote in a poem. My family may be at the end of the dock right now, looking for me.

The lines of a poem walk out to the end, and then what? They stop, weighing all possibilities. They are mathematical in their attempt to weigh, although that might not be visible on the surface. The mind lurches, trying to get traction.

"Pythagorean," by Linda Gregerson, is a good way to map this attempt:

> Square of the square of the
> root
> that holds it all together, maybe the geometricians
>
> were right. Or maybe
> it's music after all,
> the numbers in their other incarnation, makes
>
> the planets make us what we are,
> which means
> in turn

"Maybe the geometricians // were right." I am left hanging, with the word "geometricians," poised there for a couple of beats—letting it soak in on its own, without giving it value yet.

The poem is spoken by someone who has given up eating meat after seeing an ox slaughtered for food. "How strange," it says, "we need these turnings-against / / before we're allowed to see." The poem ends this way: "I don't know // what I will be or what I should call the thing / I am, / but I know what I used to be."

The poem halts and restarts. It is, as Wallace Stevens's "Of Modern Poetry," begins, "the poem of the mind in the act of finding / what will suffice." The mind stumbling along, not knowing what comes next. Gregerson's is a poem of a modern sensibility, a shared recognition of the conjunction of interior and exterior uncertainty. It cannot depend upon "what was in the script," as Stevens says; "it has to be living." Caught in the act of living. It is—and this is Stevens again—"a poem of the act of the mind."

It is a father and daughter on a becalmed sailboat, paddling a little, tacking to catch any suggestion of wind. How do we get home? Little by little as the sun goes down, the air cools more quickly than the water. Offshore breezes pick up. We watch for evidence in the rippling and point our sails to catch what we can. I am dangling my feet over the side, making little kicking motions as if I could hurry us along. I am frustrated, anxious, and angry. (He did this again! Took us too far away to get back easily.) I am delighted by the motion of my foot. I am glad to have this time alone with my father, the one I love and hate.

He broke my heart. He broke my mother's heart. He looked straight at me and couldn't see that I was only a child. His child. I was a sounding board. He lectured me on economics, science, as if I were his colleague. I couldn't get it. I had to get it so he would want to bother with me. I loved him. I could not love him because he was dangerous. His dissatisfaction, his anger, flew everywhere. You could imagine anything. Murder—or worse, leaving. He was, as I said, strong, funny, and more. Oh, lord, so much to pull a person in, only to be lost. Not an oscillation but a tension, unto breaking.

*   *   *

Lines break. And deeper inside the conch shell of a poem, the mind hears a more fundamental resistance, the stutter of consonants against the glide of vowels. Gerard Manley Hopkins, for example: listen to him taking resistance to the most exquisite extremes—the most private language, breaking itself against itself, barely able to be spoken.

> *Not, I'll not, carrion comfort, Despair, not feast on thee;*
> *Not untwist—slack they may be—these last strands*
>   *of man*
> *In me, or, most weary, cry* I can no more. *I can;*
> *Can something, hope, wish day come, not choose*
>   *not to be.*

Hopkins's rhythms are full of surprises. He *said* he was reviving the rhythms of common speech he heard in folk songs and early poems. Each line may contain any number of feet. He allows for between one and four syllables per foot, while the feet in accentual poetry (iambic, trochaic, anapestic, dactylic) normally contain only two or three. Hopkins also stressed the first syllable in each foot, so you get this breathlessness, this pushing forward—in some ways like Emily Dickinson's, but more tortured, more broken. You might think of him as bridging between the prescribed patterns of accentual verse and free verse, which follows no prescribed pattern.

Hopkins is struggling with his small canoe paddle in the middle of a great lake, looking for home. Have I left my own suffering, my loneliness, to hide inside Hopkins? Very well, I am large now. I contain multitudes.

✳   ✳   ✳

The poems my father likes have no stutters, no gaps. They tell their tender and tragic stories in splendid language. They do not make mistakes in meter to disrupt the forward movement. They do not disrupt, and in this lack of disruption they are public rather than private.

They are incantation, recitation in and/or for a collective ear. They are to be recited around the table at Willow Cottage. They are for me, sitting across from him, watching his face while he reads aloud. I do love this poem. It says what it says:

> *The wind was a torrent of darkness among the gusty trees.*
> *The moon was a ghostly galleon tossed upon cloudy seas.*
> *The road was a ribbon of moonlight over the purple moor,*
>   *And the highwayman came riding—*
> *Riding—riding—*
> *The highwayman came riding, up to the old inn-door.*

Nonetheless, even while the heart is sure of its own meter, the mind lurches. Gusts drive it in all directions. It takes skill—both practice and art—to handle the lines and rudder. Here is my father. I am stuck with him in the boat forever. When he dies I will still be stuck with him. He is the iconic presence that drives me down into myself. He is the emblem of eternal mystery, and I am a fool who will never understand.

I say to myself the end of the "Song of the Jewel Mirror Samadhi":

> *Practice secretly, working within,*
> *like a fool, like an idiot.*
> *Just to continue in this way*
> *is called the host within the host*

I say the last stanza of James Wright's "Wherever Home Is":

> *Goodbye to Leonardo, good riddance*
> *To decaying madmen who cannot keep alive*
> *The wanderers among trees,*
> *I am going home with the lizard,*
> *Wherever home is,*
> *And lie beside him unguarded*

In the clear sunlight.
We will lift our faces even if it rains.
We will both turn green.

I say to myself, by way of warning, that any writer who goes home—wherever home is—has to accept the consequence of going home, which is effacement of ego in the service of what's there, what's green. What has not turned to stone.

Fingernails, Toenails

There is a surrealist painting in the Kazuya Akimoto Art Museum, a man drawn into three portions, gathered: the eyes, the mouth, under the chin, nothing but gathers. Teeth gone, evidently. Eyes shut. A desiccation. He looks like an exotic flower, actually. I have been studying myself: my wrinkled face, my hands, that look older than I do. Swollen rivers, ridges, and pathways.

The skin dries out and wrinkles. Collagen disappears. Bones shrink in size and density, weaken, become more susceptible to fracture. Jerry, my husband, who used to be exactly my height now comes to the middle of my face. But, then, he has both scoliosis and sclerosis and has had major back surgery that added several rods and screws to straighten the mess. He does his exercises but worries more about falling. With age, muscles lose strength and flexibility.

My daughter has some gray hair, though you wouldn't know. My son's is altogether gray. What does that make me? Slow or fast, it's uphill and then the downhill. The process, it's always the process. The cane, the walker, the wheelchair, the deathbed. We joke that where we live, in a condo on the third floor, we could build a chute that would take us first next door to the high-end senior "club," then on to the assisted living building after that, then to the level-2 assisted home where my father lives, then to the nursing home down the hill, then the hospital next door to it. Stations of the human cross. I say "cross": our awareness of our aging is the suffering part.

There is an old man under the town bridge. He keeps his bottle in a brown bag: his medicine against suffering, his talisman.

There is suffering. Or can be. Jerry had a back spasm a few months ago and has been in pain ever since, first terrible pain, now less, but still. Adjust. I wouldn't say one adjusts to the surprises. At first there's surprise, then we think we'll get all better. Then we see, no, this is the condition of things. There may be a howling of anger, of sorrow, but then something else, a gap begins to reveal itself between this body, as it deteriorates, and the mind. If it has the tools, the mind can develop wisdom, philosophy, grace. I am trying for that.

It's not just Jerry. My father turned ninety-eight last week. His fingernails have become layered like shale, yellow as isinglass, too tough for scissors, though he tries. I file the jaggedness afterward. I have to press hard on the clippers to get through them. His toenails, too: layered and chitin-like. I want to use the big, tough clippers on those, but he jumps back, afraid I'll cut him. I end up filing.

His skin is delicate as a wasp's nest, dry cells flying away like moths, dark spots migrated to large ones, furry, noncancerous, the way oil gathers itself in water. His skin thins, his thoughts retract to the distant past.

He tells me Louise died. Not Louisa, the one who roams the halls and occasionally gets into his bed when he's not there. At Willow Cottage where he lives, people get weaker, they sleep more, and then one day they're gone. Every time I'm there, Louisa wanders down the hall toward us, her long gray hair in disarray, and asks, "Where are my family? Where is my brother? They should be here. Do you know where they are?" Sometimes she asks, "Where is my room?" When I open her door to show her, she says, "No, this is NOT my room. I've never seen this room in my life." I admit, I have, in exasperation, put her on the elevator to send her downstairs to find someone who "knows where her family is." Sometimes a staff person comes and temporarily steers her away.

What happened to Edgar? People go. You don't know.

Tricia smiles all the time. She wants to be kissed and hugged. The staff hugs her a lot but has to watch to see that she doesn't hug everyone else and get herself in trouble.

Generally, it's a quiet, sometimes somnolent world I enter to visit. One woman sleeps in a recliner, covered with her pink blanket almost all day. A few sit at the dinner table, as if dinner is perpetually on its way. Occasionally a burst, a confusion. One woman yells the entire time she's being given a bath.

At dinner, some of the women talk softly together. It's all men at my father's dinner table: John probably has had a stroke by the way he holds his cup in both hands and uses special utensils for eating. He smiles most of the time as if someone told him a joke. Sometimes he emerges from his confusion and reports a perfectly coherent fact. He's not entirely gone, by any means. Recently he's decided to grow a goatee. Dave is gracious and quiet, nicely dressed. He smiles amiably down the table and will answer an occasional question. My father wears a bib because he's so messy. No, not quite accurate. They put a bib by his plate and ask him each time if he'd like to wear it. No, not a bib. A "cover-up," they call it. "We are all about dignity here," said the director on his first day.

The plastic tablecloths have flowers for spring, and on the tables, little plastic bouquets, bright yellow, red, and purple. It is not a sad place. This is what I want to say. What I want to learn. It's gentle and mellow. It's like being just underwater, little minnows of thought, of brightness, of speech, breaking the surface of the deep sway now and then.

> LEAR: "You see how this world goes."
> GLOUCESTER: "I see it feelingly."

Those who stumble, who aren't sure where they are, who they are, clutch their caregivers, pleading for another cup of tea, another cookie, a trip to the bathroom, anything to feel looked after. One picks at the tablecloth.

"None is so old as those who have outlived enthusiasm," said Thoreau. My father, for the most part, is one of the enthusiasts, still. He

can no longer type a line without so many mistakes that his long trea-
tises on the fate of the economy are almost unreadable. But he bangs
along anyway. He says, "Oh, heck," and I understand the weight of
that, a man who designed and built sailboats, who has fixed clocks and
watches with exacting dexterity. He keeps up with the news.

What makes the difference between my father and the others?
My father and Jerry, twenty-four years younger, whose spine is frail
already? Molecules, mostly. David Sinclair, a Harvard Medical School
professor of genetics, led a study that found that a series of molecular
events enable communication inside cells between the nucleus and
mitochondria. As communication breaks down, aging accelerates. But
if you administer a particular molecule naturally produced by the
human body, communication can be restored in the network. In mice.
They get younger. "The aging process we discovered is like a married
couple," said Sinclair. "When they are young, they communicate well,
but over time, living in close quarters for many years, communication
breaks down. . . . And just like with a couple, restoring communication solved the problem."

People age at such vastly different rates that by the time they reach
eighty or ninety, their birth dates are entirely irrelevant. Efforts to alter
our fate are legion. Think of Dorian Gray, Gilgamesh, and Franken-
stein. They might have had more success if they'd been contemporary
worms. By manipulating the genes of a worm, scientist Cynthia Ken-
yon was able to increase its lifespan by ten times.

The person with the longest confirmed life span is Jeanne Clement,
who lived to be 122 and died in 1997. She met Van Gogh. She was
still riding her bicycle everywhere until 100. She was around to see the
internet. When my father was born, there were very few cars and rutted
dirt roads. He's lived to see travel to the moon and Mars.

He was working on a jigsaw puzzle when I got to Willow Cottage,
making perfectly rhythmic popping noises with his lips. He does this
lately. It bothers me, but he doesn't know he's doing it. He's not aware of
a lot of things. He may have been born to live a long time, but he was also
born with this mind-glitch, I'll call it that. A puzzle piece of the mind

missing. "I don't think like other people. They're a rather complicated form of animal life." He says this during his ninety-eighth birthday party.

Seven puzzle pieces are missing—no, seven pieces do not fit. So many of the pieces are so alike that no one can figure which place to wedge them into. He is determined as he was years ago to fix the furnace, but the puzzle has been stamped by machine and there is no way to rectify that.

I work on his nails, slivers of moons.

His teeth are down to stumps, aslant as the bite made them. The animal self refuses to be ignored. It hangs on, shaping itself to pressure, making a memory in the enamel. Does everything store its memory in its form? Is memory form, or is form, memory? The self as we know it seems to require the energy of memory. But what about the soul, that smoking field of self, as if from a fire meant to clear the way? Devastation. De-vast. Where is memory in that? What, if anything, lives on?

Our cells carry a memory of how to be, what to be. In the 1940s, Conrad Wadington, an English embryologist, proposed that cells acquire their identity just as humans do—by letting nurture (environmental signals) modify nature (genes). For that to happen, Waddington concluded, an additional layer of information must exist within a cell—a layer that hovers, ghost-like, spirit-like, above the gene. This layer would carry the "memory" of the cell, recording its past and establishing its future, making its identity and its destiny but permitting that identity to be changed if needed. He termed the phenomenon "epigenetics"—above genetics.

You can see it in ants. Sibling ants in their larval stage become segregated into different types based on environmental signals. Their genomes are nearly identical, but the way the genes are used—turned on or off—determines whether an ant becomes a worker, a queen, or what. In that sense, we ourselves are computers, switching on and off our Xs and Os. The brain itself is malleable, we now know. If I study the violin, my brain changes. If I am sent to assisted living, my brain changes. I adapt to that hive, find my place within it. Even my memory changes each time I recall.

If you wring out a towel in outer space, the water will hover just at the surface of the towel, not going away because there's no gravity to hold it down. Just hovering. Emerson might have called it the Oversoul. You could call it the gap of wisdom. Wallace Stevens and my grandfather might call it the imagination. My grandfather once guest-preached a sermon for the Unitarian Church in which he theorized that when our cerebral cortex got larger, we became able to imagine—to project—just beyond ourselves: a soul, a God, a heaven. Or, rather, we became smart enough to design for ourselves a way out of trouble.

Yet Hindu philosophers have long described the experience of "being" as a web—*jaal*. Which sounds like "jail" and conjures up the image of a person caught like a fly in a spider's web. Not projecting, but immersed in. We're composed of causes and conditions coming together at this momentary juncture, passing away as quickly. If this is so, where is the soul? Is anything continuous? Are we being born and disappearing all the time?

Photo of my father in front of his birthday cake, all three daughters behind. You can tell I'm the oldest, there in the center, the one with power of attorney and power of nail- and ear-hair clipping, my hands placed proprietarily on his shoulders. Photo only in digital form, light designed by Xs and Os. When he's gone there will be memory. But remember, memory shifts. It isn't reliable. The fingernails grow, but they're never the same fingernails I cut last time. They're running out of good cells to work with, growing more brittle, more shale-like. Too late for the benefit of those magic restorative molecules.

Religion thinks of the soul as a thing's inner identity, its raison d'être. Our bodies are musical instruments playing the soul's notes within us, God's intent and vision in making us. When the instrument is worn out, the soul is released into the grand mixture, and in some religions, will reappear in a new embodiment. In others, it will hover grandly with the saints and all the heavenly hosts.

My father has no religion. He worries sometimes that Everyone Else may be right, but he sticks to his guns because the other makes no sense. The body lives; the body dies. The genes, some of them, get to continue in the three daughters, their children. What part of the genes is continuous with all that switching on and off?

"Some say the world will end in fire / Some say in ice," wrote Robert Frost. If the universe is flat, it may expand forever. On the other hand, the increasing density of dark energy may cause the universe to disintegrate into unbound elementary particles and radiation: a singularity, into infinity.

It's hard to think about consciousness going away. Possibly the universe is conscious, itself. If not, where did consciousness come from and where does it go? Where has Louisa's family gone? Where is her home? Where are the particles of her being when they're no longer available to her? Where will the dozens of poems my father can recite go when he's gone? Will Alfred Noyes's "The Highwayman" continue to exist when no one can repeat "The moon was a ghostly galleon tossed upon cloudy seas"?

There they are, a sacred trinity of metaphors: the sea, the tossing, and the galleon. Three elements, the sea being the vastness, maybe heading toward a singularity; the tossing waves being the energy naturally embodied in the vastness; the third, me, here, now, filing his nails to keep them from snagging on his shirt. The relation of my thinking self to his nails, taking them on one by one, riding their crests like a galleon. The relation of my thinking self to Jerry as I rub his back at night, to ease the pain. Me, Jerry's back, pain.

If the universe is conscious, maybe its consciousness didn't come from anywhere and isn't going anywhere. No such thing as aging, in that sense. It's probably been juggling the three balls in the air forever. I think it must not get tired because it is both the juggler and the balls juggled.

Later, my father calls and wants to know what can be done with those birthday balloons. They've brought them to his room. One is deflating, he says, as if this fact is evidence of the confusion of having to deal with humans. They bring you balloons. They follow you with them. They are like speech balloons, held up for a while with helium, but then gradually not good for much. It was the gesture, though. He would not sneeze at that. He was all smiles at that.

Crown of Thorns

1.

I take him outside in his wheelchair because the sun is shining at last and it is in the forties. I put on his blue knit cap and gray fleece jacket and wrap his plaid wool scarf around his neck. I punch the exit code and he helps push his chair over the slight ridge of the doorway. I pull hard to keep him from a downhill rush before we turn a flatter corner. Every time, I think "You can't do this, yourself, anymore, with your back." He had a bad night, he says. He waited two hours before he asked for something for the anxiety. The nerves twitch. Of course it's the pain in the leg that's been removed, which goes to show the pain is in the mind, which is no comfort. People swear pain comes from some mechanical malfunction even with clear evidence of the mind's entanglement. We think that means we don't have "real" pain, that somehow real pain would be inflicted, an outside force. We think we're guilty of complicity if we connect pain to the mind.

2.

We think we're guilty of complicity if we connect pain to the mind. My mother had gold salts treatments for her arthritis. I've told you that. I asked her if she thought the fact that my father had lost his job and we were having to move and I was pitching a fit about leaving my boyfriend and my high school in my senior year, if that had anything to do with her pain. "I didn't think about it," she said. When my grandmother was told I was going to return to my hometown and get married at seventeen, she had to get the doctor to come out and give her a shot to lower her blood pressure. Sometimes the mind is clearly the culprit. Or was I the culprit? Or my parents? Or was I pregnant, as my grandmother's maid assumed? My grandmother was quick to disabuse her of that thought. That possibility was another layer of anguish, a socially constructed embarrassment.

3.

The present administration is another layer of anguish, a socially constructed embarrassment. Since Kelly started her therapy practice in DC, she's seen her work clearly attuned to the political climate—a sharp uptick of people seeking therapy for their mental anguish over Trump's policies. Can she help them relate their suffering to childhood events that left them feeling out of control? The fact is, we do not have control. The mind cannot actually a heaven of hell make. Buddhists say there are two "worlds," the relative one where our hard work to improve the world may pay off, and the absolute one that sees the vast space within which the turmoil takes place. The turmoil is also the space and the space is also the turmoil. But until the space is seen, the mind/body is laminated to the turmoil and suffers. If I tell that to you when you hurt, I deserve to get punched.

4.

If I told him that, when he hurts, I would deserve to get punched. We are going nowhere, his one foot propped on the detachable footrest. We are weaving around the paved paths, across the tiny bridge over the small bubbling creek. I imagine being him, how even this ordinary sight is a big deal, being so cooped up. Dying for many people is tediously slow. He asks the name of a tree with dangling fronds. It looks dead this time of year, so, without leaves or needles, I can't say. I admire his curiosity, which has never let up. I tell him this is an arboretum, that these trees have all been deliberately planted to provide a wide variety. He quotes Robert Louis Stevenson: "The world is so full of a number of things, I'm sure we should all be as happy as kings." When we turn back toward Willow Cottage, he's clearly relieved to recognize his home. He mostly prefers to be where he feels safe. Dying is also frightening.

5.

Dying is also frightening. The grand old Italianate buildings here not yet renovated look like a ghost town, a horror movie, with most of the windows broken out, plastic over some. They used those huge cranes to stretch plastic over the roofs last fall, to save the interiors. The cupola on top of one is rotted, but still intact, to be able to model a new one after. We live in the middle of a massive project. *All things fall and are built again. And those that build them again are gay.* Yeats heard the tragic joy, the music struck from the tension between. The stretching of strings, the compression of the squeezing, which might be called a suffering, required to make music. You my dear husband said to me you're falling apart, your back, your gut. I said when there is so much falling apart it's hard to see the raising up. It sounded too much like a sermon, but I meant that collapse exists only in reference to its opposite. It was too early in the morning, I admit. The day needs to develop from the specific, the cup of coffee, to the abstract, what we talk about over an evening glass of wine. I suspect the abstract is a way to escape what we're in the middle of.

6.

I suspect the abstract is a way to escape what we're in the middle of. "There is no coming to consciousness without pain. People will do anything, no matter how absurd, in order to avoid facing their own Soul. One does not become enlightened by imagining figures of light, but by making the darkness conscious."—C. G. Jung. Time itself is an abstraction. The image of a watch comes to mind, ticking off the artificially constructed minutes as a scrim over what just is.

7.

The image of a watch comes to mind, ticking off the artificially constructed minutes as a scrim over what just is. A lifesaving scrim, you could say. He has epoxied the face of the watch to be able to see the numbers. He said it had gotten cloudy with age, and now it is yellow with epoxy. I bought him a new battery, and after much prying he has gotten the old one out and the new one positioned properly. The time was a minute off, but after he wiggled the battery in its housing, time miraculously corrected itself. He has two other watches, plus a wall clock and a Windsor clock, all anciently ticking away, accurate because of his constant tinkering. He has wrapped the end of the Windsor's pendulum with wires and screws and nails to weight it. Something to do with age and why it now requires this weight but once didn't. Time is not the issue. To say the time, to feel the time is correct, is a footing in the roiling universe. To align the time with Greenwich is to adjust one's step to the others, to march properly, to remain a part of the human race, to keep up, for now.

8.

To march properly, to remain a part of the human race, to keep up, for now, is what we all long for, in our way. Frida Kahlo's painting *The Broken Column* shows her exposed spine as a broken, mechanical-looking column. It was painted the year I was born. She is held together with white braces, and nails are stuck randomly all over her body. Toward the end of her life Kahlo was in constant pain. Her right foot became gangrenous; part of her leg later had to be amputated. I did not use the word "suffering" until I was getting old myself, because it is a decidedly grown-up word, grand and dignified. A child doesn't *suffer* so much as she *hurts*. "Suffer" gathers up the mind into the entirety of human history and attaches the exact and specific body to it, thereby becoming holy, complete in that way. Christ *suffered*. There is a cleansing in the word because of the consciousness of itself as connected to the whole.

9.

There is a cleansing in any word because of the consciousness of itself as connected to the whole. He has been reading my poetry. "What is the difference between free verse and prose?" he asks. He is really trying to understand. A sense of it has to be transmitted, not explained. "Condensed language," I say, "line breaks," I say, not convincing even myself, having nothing to say on the subject, really, like trying to explain God to a lawnmower, the ravaging of the grass itself being meaningless without some attitude behind it. Plato didn't like poetry because he said it's imitation, and imitation pushes us farther from forms, when we already live among imitations, shadows of the real thing. The Willow Cottage elevator has a poster inside that says, "Today, give a stranger one of your smiles. It might be the only sunshine he sees all day." "Smile" = "sunshine" offers multiple depths of connection and thus might be a kind of poem, but I don't say this to him.

10.

Multiple depths of connection may be a kind of poem, but I don't say this to him. I came from him, yet he is unknowable to me. My images, what I remember, float loose, unattached to him. Nothing I remember is stored in his mind. Nothing is ever seen the same by two memories, but most parents and children can look each other in the eye and see their mind's memories converge. But not with him. There is a loneliness on both ends that's tender in its helplessness. What is seen without words is what's missing. Not the actual visual memory but an invisible *knowing* that interpenetrates the visual and is itself a part of it. What if I said that when I am sitting in church it is as if I am at the center of the universe, its energy core? The priest says the story of Lazarus must be taken for fact, not metaphor only. He says that because he thinks Plato is still involved, insisting on a form beyond our shadows. It's comforting to fasten things down. Metaphor is less satisfying than putting your arms around someone, I admit. I have no object in mind when I say "energy core," yet the feeling is deeply satisfying.

11.

I have no object in mind when I say "energy core," yet the feeling is deeply satisfying. It is like music. Rachmaninoff's Variation on a Theme of Paganini has that gorgeous haunt of notes, TA-da-da-da-DAH-duh, that I can hear immediately in my representation here, but someone who has never heard it couldn't get any pleasure out of what I've written. *O the mind, mind has mountains; cliffs of fall.* Hopkins tried to make his own despair visible in his poem. I can't feel the pain in your back, my dear. I am so sorry your back is such a mess. The two surgeries have helped, but there is still pain. Your pain is real, yet I can't feel it. In one sense, there are cliffs of fall between what you feel and what I feel. Yet it enters me as the daily news enters me. I fill myself with poetry and music as antidote. Or poetry and music are carried within the pain. Whitman and I contain multitudes:

> *What is it then between us?*
> *What is the count of the scores or hundreds of years*
>   *between us?*
> *Whatever it is, it avails not—distance avails not, and place*
>   *avails not.*

12.

Distance avails not, and place avails not. When he was still in Missouri and I told him about my chemotherapy and radiation, he heard what I said. Who knows what he understood? Maybe I didn't say enough or say it right. I tried to be brave. My fear is more abstracted now. Trying to recall nausea is almost impossible unless there's a trigger, a smell or a taste. There is so much misery in the world, to see it requires intimacy with the smallest details, touching their crust, their inflammations. I took photos of your back so you could see the puckers, the stitches. So you could believe in the full extent of what happened while you were sedated. Nothing happens in the macro sense. It is all stitches so small you have to squint. You're always after me to wear sunglasses. I'm careless in the bright light as if I have to take the full force. It is all so beautiful, even if it burns my retinas. I have to say so. I keep talking while I'm pushing him in his wheelchair because the sun is shining at last and it is in the forties.

Nothing Has Happened Yet

Nothing has happened yet. Things keep happening, a small case of pneumonia, more violently shaking fingers every week as my father tries to turn pages, but he has not succeeded at dying. When the pneumonia came on, the nurse called to remind me that he'd signed the form to have no extraordinary effort made to keep him alive, and I said, okay, but I know how he is, and so we ordered the nebulizer and antibiotics. That is, I went personally to the drug store, stood there for half an hour to get the information because I'd rushed out without his Medicare and his supplemental insurance cards. Then I ended up buying the nebulizer because it was only one-third the cost we'd have paid if we got it through insurance.

There's no need to rush, I told myself on the way to the pharmacy. Yet when dying is involved, a profound sense of urgency takes over, almost against our will. When a person's old, when we can't save them, when they don't want to be saved, even, there's this breathless urgency. Not much time left. To do what? Suddenly living becomes everything. Every gesture.

I admit, I freely admit, that when I thought he might be dying I was first sad, or maybe mostly disoriented, and then a great relief began to well up. When I was twelve, maybe, he chloroformed a litter of kittens in a big kitchen pot because he wouldn't pay to have our cat spayed and didn't want to keep the kittens. What do you do, you're a kid, and craziness seems normal because it's your life? I ran as far away as I could get, across the street, through the culvert.

I am running from him; I am still running. I am also pulled back like a rubber band.

I am running away from my brother and his twenty-four years of grand mal seizures. I am running away from his spit, his blood, his diapers, his sweet smile, the way he rocked toward me when I came in. I am running from what love has required of me. I am running from my sad mother. I am running from my first marriage, my second, from the awfulness. I am running from my beloved husband's multiple back surgeries. No wonder my chiropractor shakes his head.

I am running from my own mind. For over thirty years, I've been sitting on my cushion every morning, and longer times when I can, to see the space between me and my raging thoughts. This is the space, too, this page. This fury of words.

Running charged with both fear and anger. Charged with. As in building up a charge based on continual friction—bearings, electricity, magnetism—the round that drives the whole of being. Including anger. This morning we got a call from the owner of our storage unit. Something sticky had leaked through from the just-vacated unit next to ours. Little annoyances, big ones. What goes round.

Also, my father called this morning to tell me once again he had terrible dreams. He said he was riding his bicycle somewhere that he realized was too far away to get to by bike, and he had promised to meet his childhood friend, Hal Stevens, somewhere, too far away to get there by bike. And he had two heavy passengers on the bike with him. He was peddling as fast as he could. "How did you feel about this?" I asked. "Terrible, exhausting, hopeless," he said.

Everything we're taught is about living; nothing about dying. I watch my father die slowly. I watch with curiosity how the aging mind runs down. His is remarkably sharp for ninety-nine, but he is mixing up his daughters sometimes, and when he first wakes up, he hardly knows where he is. It's as if the body is settling into its last sleep and has to be roused day after day to create its personality all over again. Even I sometimes get up a little tired of the same old life, same old thing, the work of creating a self out of the daylight world.

Get up, put on the same sweats, pull out the same yoga mat, do the same stretches, then light my candle, sit on the cushion, get up, eat breakfast.

I notice he is never hungry. He eats because he's in the habit of eating what's put in front of him, but he has no interest in it. Where he lives, residents are encouraged to eat and drink. There are two glasses at each place at the table, water and juice, milk and juice, or juice and juice. There's afternoon "tea," with cake and cookies.

I am sitting in Cuppa Joe's with my laptop, watching people drinking coffee. These are the ones in the middle of this life, or somewhere before the deep slope begins. Most have gray hair, like mine. What are they doing? One is making a list, three are talking with their hands, planning. The movement of hands is a gathering and an organizing, beyond the words, shoring up the words. There are the hands gesticulating, there is laughter. And there is music, another kind of voice, another level. The bearded guy is chopping behind the counter. The woman with pink hair and a pink pony tattoo on her arm takes my money. Her voice is remarkably high and piercing, like a child's, but sweet. It is mid-morning, which is why most people here are old. They are not at work. I am increasingly aware, at my age, of the trajectory of life.

People close to dying sometimes have a period of profound awareness. They see spirits, they know they're about to die, and they feel happy to be changing dimensions. If this is "all in the mind," maybe everything else is, too. We conjure up our sense of what's true.

Some people become agitated before death. My father has those bad dreams. He says he doesn't want to go to bed at night because of them, and also, he feels "bad" in some undefined way. He feels sure it's connected with dying but dying never quite happens. All his life, of course, he's been fascinated by religion, not believing a word of it and interested in how anyone can. He provokes discussion, still, to see if there might be something he's missed. Indeed there is, and he's smart enough to sense that he's unusual, that those around him seem to have a secret code. "I am not like other people," he says. "I don't think I'll go to hell," he says, in response to a lifetime of correspondence with his fundamentalist brother-in-law, who at this late hour desperately keeps on trying to save his soul. You can tell my father worries that if everyone else knows things he doesn't get, then maybe he's missed something here. Still, he has integrity. He stands by his declaration that religion is nonsense.

He sometimes mentions these days how difficult a child he was, how he wished there *were* a heaven he could go to and tell his parents he's sorry for the way he was. I'm thinking his rages were all part of his genetic makeup. We've tried to suggest that, to explain autism a bit, but he doesn't get it. How can you imagine emotions you've never had?

He wants to wake up dead. Above all, he wants to cease upon the midnight with no pain. It's funny, he's always been simultaneously a hypochondriac and a stoic. He could tear his knee working on a sailboat and hardly notice it. But he's poured Neo-Synephrine drops into his nose and taken antihistamines all his life, constantly complaining that he has trouble breathing. His parents had his nose checked by specialists. Nothing but nasal rhinitis. He says he's not afraid of dying; he's afraid of the pain of dying. I've said to him hundreds of times that he's most likely at his age to die suddenly of a heart attack or a blood clot, but he doesn't seem to hear that. And that there are potent drugs. He doesn't hear a lot I say. In the years just before his birth, the leading cause of death was diarrhea, or other intestinal distresses. Not far behind was tuberculosis. Pneumonia was third. A pretty grim prospect to a young boy.

Three years ago I thought I might be dying. Even today, at any time, there could be a recurrence of my endometrial cancer. Some people use the word "remission," but I don't like that, as if I'm suspended, as if the disease is holding its breath, thinking whether it will attack again. We're all dying, of course. We've been doing it all our lives. Yet all we talk about is past and future, when what's going on is this, right now. Several times I've had scary symptoms. They turned out to be nothing, but the fear surged each time. Part of the training of Thai

Forest Buddhists is to watch a human body decompose, day after day. This is what is: we are born, we die, and we decompose. It's all transition. Thailand's monks were called upon to cremate thousands of tsunami victims because they've been trained in charnel houses or by staring at photos of decomposing bodies. They can handle it.

The first time I thought the cancer might have returned, I tried a Buddhist practice. I imagined all phases of my death. I imagined the beginning of pain; I imagined the increase of it; I imagined my deep grief at leaving this life; I imagined being fuzzy with drugs; I imagined being bedridden, with no energy to get up anymore. At each stage, I stopped and put myself fully there. Oh, it's only that. Just that moment and that experience. It was so clear to me that the fear of fear is the only problem. The rest is simply what's happening.

What's happening is that I've finished my coffee. I must visit my father today. He'll tell me he had a bad night. He seems to need to tell me, first thing, about his bad night. The body, after all, has a built-in mechanism. It wants to live. It wants to live until it doesn't, which comes very close to the end, apparently. The wanting to live, the pulling toward life when life is almost gone, must be a suffering.

When I conjure up my mother, I see how thin is the veil between one person and another, how expansive the mind. I see her as I have a thousand times since, in the hospital, her brain registering nothing, according to the scans. I fit down into her body. It's me. Everyone has gone home for the night. I'm lying there in the big room reserved for the dying at the end of the corridor, perpetual fluorescent lights, hard, hard tile floors all around. I am briefly waking up from my coma, as people sometimes do just before death. What now? What should I imagine of her loneliness?

This is what death does: it offers a rounding out, an assessment. A grade at the end of the term. No wonder people talk about heaven and hell. At that moment of leaving, one can't help but go back over a life. No, that's us, the living, going back. Probably the truth is different. Probably it's hard to die and it takes one's whole attention to stay with the breaking down of components that have sustained us, to let them go, to move into the unknown. To let go of the mind's grip on what it's made of all this. My writing will be let go, released into the vastness where there's no need to differentiate.

Is God there? Father Thomas Keating, the famously enlightened monk, said that everyone uses the word "God" to mirror back at themselves what they need God to be. What they're seeing are their own concepts, their own needs. Remove the word "God" and it's possible to begin to glimpse the Ultimate Reality, or Truth, which has no name, which is incarnate in us, which *is* us, and is ungraspable with the intellect alone. And, he says, is entirely loving, because everything is dependent upon everything else for its existence. We are loved the way a hand loves its fingers. Try telling my father that.

My first death was my first husband's father, a little man, funny and smart, chain smoker, drinker, and a favorite of mine. He had lung cancer. He grew thinner; then he was unable to get up. The sofa bed in the living room was made up so that visitors could come. I have one memory only. I had come to see him. I was maybe twenty-five. I didn't know what to say. No one had mentioned death, people often didn't then, so it remained a pea-soup fog in the air. He was white, ravaged. I sat there awhile, on the edge of the bed. What did I say? I don't know. Then it was time to leave. He looked at me as I got up. There was an exchange of such depth, everything unsaid. Was it love, was it goodbye, was it some summation of our lives as we knew each other? Would it have been better to say something? To have words to remember? Should death have been talked about?

Once we were at the donut shop he and my mother-in-law owned. I was sitting at the office desk. To the right and a little behind me was my husband, making sandwiches for the little business we had on the side, to pay our way through school. I reached back and grabbed his leg, high up. Just playing. Oh, no! It was my father-in-law! I blushed. We laughed. The moment was so rich, a level of unspoken ironic comedy his own tense son wouldn't have been capable of. So much cannot be said, yet the world stumbles on trying to say something that approximates the truth.

*   *   *

Over two thousand years ago, the Greek philosopher Epicurus observed
that the art of living well and the art of dying well were one. Every
magazine I read at the beauty salon tells me how to live well, but how
does one die "well"? A man I knew in Delaware, a well-known musi-
cian, a gentle, kind man, devout Episcopalian, thrashed, cursed, fought
like hell in his last hours. Was this "bad"? Was he expunging repressed
demons at the end? Across town, his lifelong friend died in his sleep
the same night. Scheduled for major heart surgery the next day without
disclosing the alcoholism that would have complicated the surgery,
he simply seemed to decide to die, right then. Was a good death? The
answer may be the same as to the question of "Who is God?" To ask
at all is to shine a mirror back at our own preconceptions.

My father calls to say he's dying. He feels strange when he's lying
down. For the hundredth time, he says, "I don't know what you'll do
with all this stuff in my room." Jerry and I are in the middle of a movie.
I would put my phone on "do not disturb," but you never know. I tell
him that we can take care of his things, no problem.

I wrote that I'm angry, didn't I? I think I misunderstood the emotion. I thought it was an emotion, and I called it anger, when it was
more likely a propulsion—call it love, even, toward the intense and
glorious details of living. That fierce desire is also a suffering. Electric:
the kind that holds atoms together. When the force is no longer strong
enough, the atom breaks apart, and the energy that went into holding it
together is released, like flames, like smoke. The energy isn't running
away, then, but becoming something that looks like something else.
At some point, we call it death, or we call it birth. That depends upon
where we stand. And when.

Even words. They get born somehow from various elements,
then disperse, gradually, from lack of use. Like Cuppa Joe's, where
I am now, the name born maybe from a shortening of "cup of

'jamoke'"—from java and mocha, which is what the 1931 military manual says. Or maybe it's a drink to be enjoyed by an ordinary "joe." World War I soldiers called instant coffee from the G. Washington Refining Company a "cup of George," or "Geo," which maybe turned into "Joe." Meanwhile, who cares but me, parsing the sign on the door to see what's underneath.

Midway on his life's journey, Dante found himself in a dark wood. His was the spiritual dilemma of midlife that still has the luxury of finding its way out, using the tools of language, looking up answers in Wikipedia, studying scripture, philosophizing. Long past the mid-point, it seems that the mind opens back down into the etymology of its existence. It remembers who we hurt, who loved us, who we loved, before words laminated themselves to the raw feeling. The mind begins to dis-solve the dilemmas. Somehow we sense, even if there's turmoil, the sweetness inherent in both living and dying, sugar stirred into coffee, enough sugar so that it tastes a little like dessert.

Taking Care

I take off my watch and crouch beside the shower stall, sleeves rolled up. Jerry reaches out and hands me the wet, soapy wash-cloth. I reach in and wash his feet and up to the knees, the part he can't reach. I wash his back. When he steps out, I dry the same areas. I reapply the bandage to his incision. I gather his shoes, socks, briefs, and jeans all together. I'm a flexible seventy-three-year-old, but getting up over and over to fetch them begins to feel like calisthenics. Together we get him dressed.

The hardest part is the support hose. They have an opening at the bottom—to let the foot breathe, I guess—that has to be aligned just under the ball of the foot. I've learned I have to gather the tall sock up and get that alignment before I attempt to pull the rest over the heel. The sock is of course very tight, so wrangling it over the heel takes strength. Also, his heel, being old, is scratchy, and snags the fabric. The toe part may slip off center, in which case I have to wiggle it around. Then come his regular socks. It's especially tricky with the Smartwool ones, that fit tighter.

I get his feet through both pant legs before pulling them up high enough so he can grab them. We are going into our third month of being joined at the hip. Jerry's back brace doesn't allow him to bend or twist. Well, more like a year. A year ago is when the bad pain started. That's when I started rubbing his back every night, a deep, both-hands massage. I am still doing it, to relieve the discomfort of his wearing the brace all day. I've been through this before. Three years ago, he had his first back surgery.

After he's dressed, I wash Wally's cat dish and give him new food, I turn on the gas fireplace, I clean the litter box. I come back in the bedroom and do my stretches. I meditate. I am on a treadmill of duty. I run the errands, wash the clothes, take Jerry to the doctor. Snow is heaped on the cars. I clean off the snow. My brother-in-law is in the hospital. I visit him. My father is nearby in an assisted living facility. I am his chief go-to person. I visit.

I have been mostly gentle and sympathetic, haven't I? But sometimes it feels as if I'm turned inside out, hollowed out, everything by necessity turning toward the next task. Sometimes it feels robotic—get out the bandages, the washcloth, the towel. Put them on the bed. Wash the incision, dress it again.

When Jerry had his first back surgery at the University of Michigan Medical Center, I walked down the hall past a hospital room where a nurse or an aide was feeding a bedridden patient. Just a glance in. The patient was old, obviously barely alive. The nurse could have shoveled the food in while daydreaming or staring out the window, but her entire attention was on the patient. The expression on her face was sheer love, sheer tenderness, as if the meaning of her life was to feed this person.

Recollected. The mind returned to its present activity, rather than scattered. St. Teresa of Avila taught the practice of "recollection"—i.e., keeping the senses and the intellect in check and not allowing them to stray from the object of meditation. "God is within," she said she learned from St. Augustine.

I sit at my computer, plowing down into my own personal mind. I don't want to let myself skate across the top of my ego, which would like to assert itself everywhere, but to look hard. Come back here, Fleda. Stay with these damn support hose. This beloved and sometimes irritating incapacitated person. Don't turn away. How does Jerry feel about his helplessness? Well, helpless. Stuck. Yet here we are, a teeter-totter of kindness/irritation, but not a stable one, since we know this situation is temporary. It's shifting every day.

St. Teresa's modern-day namesake, Mother Teresa: How many hours did she spend in prayer? Probably not many. On she went to the next task. She must have been sustained by the thought that her work was God's work. Since all good work could be said to be divine work, I guess dressing Jerry is, too. A kind of faith, since what is faith but a sense that what we do is exactly what needs to be done, that the doing itself is sacred? Call it love, or call it necessity, when the work is there in front of you, and you're the one who's able to do it, most of the time, most of us just do it.

Then, too, I'm trying to figure what the "personal" is. I see my mother bent over my brother's bed. He is nearly twenty by then, severely brain-damaged, no longer able to walk, needing his diapers changed, needing feeding. Her hands severely arthritic, she sat on a tall kitchen stool, which enabled her to reach down instead of up, to put the spoon in his mouth. She talked to him. He heard her sounds, her tone, if nothing else. Oh, I see now why I was moved by the nurse! It was my mother I was seeing.

All my young life, there was Markie to take into account, to watch for, to catch if he started to have a seizure. I was dying to leave home, but there was my mother, who couldn't. There are legions who can't. They take care. That is what they do. Some are happy, some sad, some angry, some like robots, resigned.

Here's another way I see this: men in department stores, dragged there by their wives, sitting on benches, waiting. There is a resignation that is also no doubt love. Patience. The job of just sitting there. The job of being stuck in this life, no way out of this love and annoyance.

My mother is more clear to me, all these years since her death. I used to say it felt as if she wasn't there, her presence was so timid, so malleable, next to my father's force. But I recall her personal self now, the way she licked her lips, the way she lifted a cup of coffee, pinkie in the air. I hear her clear her throat, her struggle to be heard, to find what to say. I hear her clear her throat in the mornings, always phlegmy. I see the thin, worn band of her wedding ring, her delicate fingers, her tentative touch. Oddly, the broad scope of my father's personhood is felt more as waves of energy, not as exactness of detail. Yet both are hollowed out, formed into memory, with its reckless slippages. I am stuck with the memories.

I am also stuck with my resistances. I do not want to be held down by sickness. Been there already. I had cancer. I have, as far as it goes, recovered. From my childhood, too. I have felt trapped in marriages that were all wrong, all wrong. Not this one, but this one has come with accessories: aging, pain, disabilities.

Also, don't you know, I am stuck in the United States of America as it roils and boils into some new thing? I am married to it, no matter that it appears to have grown fat and self-centered and mean. I didn't know that the seeds of this were there all along. I thought we had a good relationship, I thought I could overlook the cracks and fissures because of the good. I thought—I guess I really did—that we were happy. Now I am plodding along, day by day, as astounded as if I had just discovered I was married to an addict. How could I have not seen the signs, the red eyes, the shift in temper, the money missing from the sock drawer? How does one live with this? What are the boundaries beyond which love cannot go, beyond which I risk losing myself?

Why was the great Russian poet Osip Mandelstam sent to Siberia to die? Partly because he wrote a poem calling Stalin a cockroach, but mostly because of his poems, in general.

"Only in Russia is poetry respected, it gets people killed. Is there anywhere else where poetry is so common a motive for murder?" Mandelstam wrote.

The political poems were incendiary, true, but wait, the damnable issue was poetry itself, its personal nature, when the government required art to be in the service of the state. Writing about one's anguish, anger, jealousy, about birds and trees as objects apprehended by a single, unique consciousness, was seen to undermine the great marching mechanics of the Whole.

Furthermore, can one be Black, and/or gay, and not Be that in the poem? Carl Phillips writes in "A Politics of Mere Being": "At no point did I think of myself as having an agenda that could be called political. Rather, my agenda, to the extent that it can even be called that, has always been to speak as honestly as possible to my own experience of negotiating and navigating a life as myself, as *a* self—multifarious, restless, necessarily ever-changing as the many factors of merely being also change—in a world of selves."

Does the self, holding still, primarily observe and report? Does the self primarily act? Mother Teresa was utterly absorbed in giving her life in service to the Whole. Her individual self was apparently held entirely in the arms of that larger Self. For her, no poetry, no distance, no watching a flower slowly open. For her, the urgency of the moment.

I'm not Mother Teresa, I'm pretty sure. My particular qualities are as inherent in my being as Carl Phillips' gayness and Blackness is in his. In all my years of writing, I have never before been compelled to so closely scrutinize my need to write. I have never before examined the word "selfish" with such disinterest. Self-ish. Belonging to, having the characteristics of the self. Overly concerned with self. How much is "overly?" Is it my "self" that I'm so concerned with? Fame and fortune aside, still I want to shut my door, get on with the writing, not even knowing what I want to write about. "About" isn't the point. Just as a painter begins with paint and sees only later what she might have been intending, I begin with words and see later what they might be adding up to.

I am writing about washing my husband's back. I am writing about helping my father work his jigsaw puzzle. These are the atoms, yet surely the atoms will take a shape that needs to be seen. By whom? Who is my audience? Am I simply standing on stage, red baseball cap pulled down, mouthing whatever seems to draw the loudest cheers? Am I visiting the sick, taking care of the wounded, signing a hundred petitions, in order to fill in the outline of someone I would like to be, someone who might therefore draw cheers from God and all well-meaning folk?

I look down as far as I can into this. I see my gut inclinations, I see the stories I've cooked up about my childhood, my divorces, my cancer. I see the gradual curvature of a life like the gradual curvature of Jerry's spine. Once the inclination begins, it reinforces itself. The weight pulls one way, and that way becomes the Way. The poem I wrote in sixth grade, the journal I kept in junior high, the class I took in creative writing in college, the prize I won. It all began to feel inevitable.

Jerry's spine, in spite of surgery, is not going to be straight. It has never been straight. When I met him, he walked with his trunk bent forward. Gradually, parts of the unbalanced body began to cry out at the unnatural weight they were asked to carry. The hip went. Then the lumbar area. Then the thoracic. At night I rub my hand down the ridge that's developed along the surgical area. Bone grows around the rods and screws and before long, it's all one organism. A sad sight in daylight. But it functions. He has less pain, more ability to walk. We are all deformed, of course. The tilt of the earth off-center is responsible for the seasons. The deformities are our personality, our character.

If I were the one leaning to the crowd in my red MAGA baseball cap, I would be following the path of least resistance. Love me. Love what you think is me. Love these words, which are really your words I was clever enough to put in my own mouth. I would obliterate my true nature, to get this love. Mother Teresa did the same, you could say. She, however, kept her eye on an aspiration so large that she was absorbed into it: save all beings. What is, then, my true nature? Anyone's true nature? If I wish to be myself, an individual, don't I need to know my true nature, my foundation-nature? My soul. What is true of me, before the additions.

Before the additions? Impossible to say what that might be. The incorporeal essence of me? That which lasts eternally, but is somehow, in some way, still "me"? Ridiculous on one level, but, still, I write with the conviction that my unique way of seeing, my angle, through the filter of my consciousness, is worth finding words for. That the flutter of my words can shift the air a thousand miles away.

Today is freezing cold, the ground covered with a foot of snow, yet the sun is shining, illuminating spangles still blowing and falling. We have gotten Jerry dressed. He is sitting in the one chair that's comfortable for him, reading the paper. I am at my desk, with a cup of green tea beside me. Our souls surely are not located in in some mystical realm, but right here, embedded in these actions, these reasonable observations. The Greek philosophers felt that the soul must have a logical faculty, the exercise of that faculty being the most divine act of being human. St. Thomas Aquinas argued that all living beings, vegetative and sensitive (animal), as well as human, have souls, but humans alone are capable of acquiring intellectual, or "spiritual," knowledge as well, and of choosing to freely act toward chosen ends.

Think about it. If the soul is going to do anything worth doing, it must not be a loose cannon. Instead of flitting around with its mystical spangles, it must be logical. It must, first of all, see clearly, and then act on what it sees. It must see climate change and act to alleviate it. It must see human suffering, recognize its own kindred suffering, and take logical steps toward remedy.

Claude McKay's poem "I Know My Soul" begins, "I plucked my soul out of its secret place, / And held it to the mirror of my eye, / To see it like a star against the sky." To locate the soul requires order, for example, the order of his poem. There must be discipline. Mustn't there? Mustn't we have bells and candles, kneeling and chants, meter and rhyme and line breaks, scriptures and exams, thrust and drag, unblinking absorption in illuminating a manuscript, or in the painting of a perfect *enso*? An *enso*, a circle drawn in one brushstroke, is only possible when the mind is so trained that it knows how to be free, no longer caught by what-ought-to-be, but at that moment free to let the body follow, to express absolute enlightenment, strength, elegance: the perfectly tuned universe.

Did we think Whitman a loose cannon, loafing and inviting his soul, completely at ease, observing a spear of summer grass? Yet in that ease he forms a careful logic, a history. He places himself within a continuum. The creeds and schools are merely held in abeyance. He doesn't forget them even when he steps beyond them, allowing nature to speak "without check with original energy":

> *My tongue, every atom of my blood, form'd from this soil, this air,*
> *Born here of parents born here from parents the same, and*
>   *their parents the same,*
> *I, now thirty-seven years old in perfect health begin,*
> *Hoping to cease not till death.*
>
> *Creeds and schools in abeyance,*
> *Retiring back a while sufficed at what they are, but never*
>   *forgotten,*
> *I harbor for good or bad, I permit to speak at every hazard,*
> *Nature without check with original energy.*

Whitman knew the risks of spreading out the universe of himself. Of speaking. Oh, listen to me, dragging in Whitman! When I get to the limits of my understanding, I plow on, hoping the words might raise from my unconscious some order that my conscious mind can't yet fathom.

I'm training myself to walk slowly, beside Jerry's walker. I am a fast person. I dislike slow walking. I've often found myself five steps ahead of him, even before the walker. At the moment, I concentrate on each step. I study the shop windows. My body is a revved motor. I accept that. Someday it will be a burned-out motor, and perhaps its essence will come loose from its housing. Perhaps it will join the other essences in a vast hallelujah chorus. That will be me, the one still trying to settle down enough to stay in harmony. Actually, no, I will be the one who has no intention of settling down. But that will be okay, since every individual voice fits somewhere. There is no such thing as disharmony, on that scale.

Mortality, with Friends

Robin:* *This is really not a subject that I feel
like I can talk to non-cancer friends about.*

I lift the shoebox from the top of the closet. It feels empty. I check to make sure before I throw it away. Wrapped in tissue paper is my wig. The really quite nice wig that looked just like my hair, that Jerry and my hairdresser had helped me pick out, trimmed exactly for me, that I wore during my entire hairless time. I feel some recoil, some tightening of the gut, now, seven years later. But then, here I am, petting it like a lost kitten come home. A tenderness, an intimacy, I hadn't expected. The poor thing, what a hard time we had together. How we took care of each other.

As if one of us had died. Flashes through my head that if the cancer came back, my hair is now too gray for this wig. Flashes through my head that this time I'd just wear a scarf. Flashes through my head: this time. As if I needed to plan ahead.

You can't help this. The shock of cancer is so great your entire body has reset. It now operates on some sort of deep alert, below language. Your logic has met its match. It has learned to collude with magic.

Gail: *There is a gap between my intellectual understanding of
my situation, and deeper psychological processing. I understand*

---

* Robin and others are Facebook friends who answered my request for thoughts
about their own cancer survival.

that my recurrence odds are high, but my brain is protecting me
from fully comprehending this fact. For better or worse, I don't
go around thinking about it every minute.

I'm waiting to hear from the doctor about this year's scan. My
mind is off into another dream, triggered by the pain in my back. I've
noticed that there's not a heck of a lot of difference between awake
dreaming and asleep dreaming: there is a tumor growing on my lumbar
spine. There is cancer in my bladder, which accounts for my frequent
need to pee. The doctor has not yet called because he wants me to be
able to have a few precious hours of hope before he tells me there is
none. Or, he hasn't called because he's not good at giving bad information. He's putting it off.

I do actually have back pain. Last summer's swimming made my
back hurt. I would get a sharp catch every time I rolled over on the
dock. I attributed this to my knees. My theory was that my damaged
knees were no longer holding my body up straight, which was putting
stress on my lower back. I bought even more expensive tennis shoes. I
had my knees x-rayed. But no, it was my back. It has been so bad lately
that getting out of bed is an operation involving a slow acclimation to
the upright position, waddling to the bathroom holding on to the wall
until the pain gradually eases up.

Last winter, a torn meniscus, and also, my father died, and also,
I had hernia surgery. I was depressed, wasn't I? All winter. Then in
July I got a horrible cold that turned so bad I had to have antibiotics. It
didn't really go away for three months, until a few weeks ago. Coughing and hoarseness. Stress has caused the cancer to return.

The entire year after I was diagnosed with stage 3c endometrial
cancer, I blogged every week. I talked about the fear, the details of
treatment, my doctors, what I was doing with myself while deadly
chemicals were coursing through my body, while radiation was eagerly
wiping out both the good and the bad. It has been 7 years, or 84 months,
or 365 weeks, or 2556 days, or 3,680,640 minutes since then. Am I
"cured"? Since then three friends have died of cancer after the five-year

marker, one other is tentative. My stepdaughter Pam has stage 4 breast cancer. In a toxic world, our immune systems are gasping, sometimes gasping their last. Is it too late for everything? For the trees, the birds? I think sometimes it would be better to get hit by a truck. To wait for immediate results is almost unbearable. But long-term is another thing.

> Peggy: *Every day, I run my fingers over my breast, first before I rise from bed and later when I'm soapy in the shower. If I sleep in a way that puts pressure on the breast, the discomfort lasts for hours. I worry. Scar tissue makes it impossible to tell whether there's another jellybean of cancer growing. The oncologist's PA says, "Just be aware of anything different." I fret that I'm not perceptive enough to notice each change.*
>
> *Some medical person told me that the cancer cells are always there, but sometimes some of them go crazy. So I acknowledge what I carry. I try not to list all the possible triggers.*

I wonder if anyone knows what "living fully" means. You could head for Patagonia at last? Finally see an opera at the Met? Get married or un-married? I got up this morning, did my stretches, meditated, ate oatmeal with raisins, as always. I suppose living fully means "with awareness." I knew a woman who found out her cancer was going to be quickly terminal. She said life was wonderful, knowing how little of it was left. The increase of fear could spark the present moment. Or, the lack of fear, when there's no hope left.

> Joan: *People I know who've had, for instance, breast cancer, talk about the statistics and analyze every aspect of themselves that might make a difference. But the cancer I had is so rare, and survival so unlikely, that there aren't sufficient statistics on which to make a prediction. In a way, that's liberating.*

My oncologist told me the statistics for five-year survival for my cancer, which were dismal. "Disregard them," he said. Might as well have told me to not see an elephant when someone says "elephant." He said, though, that research is making giant strides, and these numbers were out of date already. He also said, "You are not a statistic." My brother-in-law, a mathematician, explained the difference between average and mean. It looked considerably better his way. I am past the five magical years. I have a friend who died in her sixth year.

> Linda: *My wife has had cancer six times. Only one of these was a recurrence. We don't talk much about her nine-year remission, but it's there every time we set the table. We use the prettiest dishes!*

That's the thing. One cancer can go away and another, seemingly unrelated one can pop up. If the body was a breeding ground before, what's to say it isn't still? And now it's damaged with radiation and chemotherapy, so it's more prone than ever. Green tea. Drink green tea. Eat well. Meditate. Live well. Have loving friends. Practice tightrope walking.

> Mark: *The subtle pull, as if a rat was pulling on my pant leg, is always present. Everyone says I look great, remark on my energy, make kind statements about continuing creativity, etc. But every time I have trouble swallowing (I was radiation-zapped for cancer of the tongue) or wake in the middle of the night with dry mouth or feel tired or depressed (which is rare) I think—ah! Cancer. And I know it is less likely every day that it is the cancer I came in with, and I know the statistics are ever more leaning in my favor. But there it is: cancer, the unwelcome visitor, was beaten back by very difficult treatment, but beaten? I don't know.*

Twice some small body-message convinced me the cancer had returned. The kind of convinced that feels the way it did a long time ago when I pulled out in front of the Karmann Ghia in the rain. Suddenly all is slow motion. The thinking mind shuts down and watches, almost dispassionately, the coming thud. "This is the end" doesn't arrive as a thought, more like being submerged in a wave. I carried that terror with me, not saying anything to anyone, until I couldn't carry it alone. I told Jerry, who then had cancer with me. Until we didn't, until all was well.

I'm seventy-five. I've had my share of life, I say to myself. I can feel my life, even in good health, slowly, inexorably beginning to wrap up. Spotted skin, deep rivulets of skin on my arms when I hold them up, arthritis. What if I were forty? What if I had small children, as my stepdaughter did when she was first diagnosed? That's one of the mind games. There's always someone worse off to compare to.

> Carol: *In the years I took Arimidex, it was on my mind every day—just the act of taking the pill, and the menopausal side effects kept survival on my mind. I used all the cancer insurance money to redecorate the house, something I had been putting off for years. I thought it was foolish to wait any longer. We called it my Martha Stewart phase. All the compromise beiges my ex-husband and I chose were transformed into peach, and green and even red. I redesigned a bedroom during one of my forty-five-minute MRI scans.*

You might think you'd turn toward spiritual things. You might do that. So, what's spiritual? Is prayer or meditation more spiritual than redecorating the house? All things are of the spirit, is my take on it. It's only when we separate mind and body that the precious objects go dead, quit talking to us, quit inspiring us, i.e., filling us with spirit.

No one understands spirit. Understanding is something the rational brain does. "I thought," "I thought," is what we say, after what we thought is no longer relevant and maybe never was. The mind tries desperately to organize, to settle this thing into some sort of controllable formula.

Paula: *I can't shake the irrational fear that every bump or pain or bruise means the cancer is back. It's a side effect no one really talks about.*

In the bottom of the plastic bin where I keep out-of-season clothes, I have packed four or five cancer hats. One is an absurd one a friend knitted me, green, that comes to a point like an elf's hat, and is way too big. I keep these, plus a stack of How to Eat with Cancer books. I dare not get rid of them. Joan Didion called it "the year of magical thinking," the year after her husband died. I have been reborn into the life of magical thinking. Getting rid of these artifacts would be dangerous, would tempt the gods, I think. Not think, but feel. And supplements. Who knows if supplements make a hill of beans difference? They are my communion wafers, my hedge against hell. I am living Pascal's wager.

My doctor's nurse calls. Your scan is all clear, she says. "Hooray!" I say. Even though, years back, my oncologist said he doesn't even bother to do yearly scans after the first five years, because nearly all recurrences are found through symptoms, not through scans. It's my primary doctor who wants them done. Okay. Here's the thing: I have a huge sense of relief. I am okay. Give me a scan every month. That would be okay. I would be okay every month. My mind is ravenous for facts. The doctor, the x-ray technician are scanning my scans. They are studying my scans, looking for the slightest anomaly. They have enlarged the pictures. They are tracing their fingers along the spine, along my shadowy organs. This is a fact. Nothing has been found, again.

I have to say, the scan process itself leaves plenty of time for the imagination. You are a technician of yourself, mentally tracing every peculiarity you can remember. You sit in the radiology waiting room for two hours, drinking two bottles of something clear that has contrast dye in it. Then you are called back into the room to lie on the bed that will send you into the large white tube. First the nurse tries to find a vein. Then she tries again. You've had so many needles in veins, they're full of scar tissue. Then she calls for the expert vein person. She comes with her hand-held sonogram machine that can locate veins. She uses a child-size needle and succeeds first time. She injects the other dye, the intravenous one that apparently shows up something else.

This is not you after all. This is me. Yours might be different. But they are the same in this way. You are asked to hold your breath, then release. You have been holding your breath for two hours. You have been holding your breath for a week, two weeks.

> Gail: *A pattern seems to be emerging: for several days after I get a good scan result, I feel incredibly happy, almost euphoric. When the high wears off, irritability kicks in. Little things get on my nerves. Lurking beneath the crabbiness is a simmering anger: anger that I have to be on this emotional roller coaster. Anger that these scans are part of my life from now on. Anger that this happened to me at all. Eventually the anger fades and my mood returns to its baseline—optimistic, a little worn out by life's demands—until the next scan rolls around.*

Irrational. I know it is. I know that my body does not begin cranking up cancer as scan appointment nears. I know I would have noticed something. I am noticing something. I am noticing everything. I am a walking time bomb.

I am exaggerating all this. Maybe. Don't misunderstand me: I am not terrified of dying. Dying will be okay, I think. When I was starting treatment, I finally quit being brave and started sobbing, holding Jerry as we lay in bed. I was so sad for myself, for him. I did not want to end this life. I love this life. But when I know it's over, my hunch is I will adjust without resorting to platitudes or fervent prayers for miracles.

Sure, we all started living with death when we were born. It was in us, but we were climbing uphill toward our full height, our lovely arms and legs, our desire finding itself, our intellect full of surprises. Death was in us but had nothing to say. Until it did. Then life began to glow with what you might call a gorgeous sunset light. How beautifully clothed the ending can be! Unless it isn't.

Death, or the idea of death, is like a wall. No, it's like a nothing. You can't see ahead. You've never been able to, but you could imagine. You could imagine streets of gold ahead if you wished, but you know perfectly well that's your imagination gone wild.

Where am I now? I'm writing today sitting in the auto stereo store while they install my remote car starter. Today we woke up to snow, too soon. Before Thanksgiving! I'm looking forward to being able to get in my little Prius, all warmed up for me. Here in the showroom is an old VW bug, the authentic kind my first husband and I had. I walk around it and look at its flat dashboard barely more than a foot from your face. You could slam into it in a second.

Those of us who feel the risk daily don't feel it daily. Not usually. We have remote starters installed in our cars. And, personally, I am dreaming of our old VW, with a cardboard box in the back to hold the baby. To hold Kelly, who mercifully survived without a fancy infant car seat. We have all mercifully survived this long.

Movie of the World

Our dinner partners, Ed and P.J., think it's cool that they've been paired with virgins. They themselves sign up for one cruise after another. They're leaving soon for a twenty-eight-day, and then a longer one after that. It's as cheap as staying home, they say, considering room and board, and entertainment, and medical attention if needed. I can see this. I can see endless gentle rocking, kissing the shore and moving on, a taste of everything, everyone all smiles. Our steward, Gede, has the most fulsome smile, genuine and sweet. Our servers at dinner, the same ones every night, plus the sommelier, all smiles, so glad to see us. We can do no wrong. Our wishes granted in a flash.

Granted because there are 862 crew from 45 countries on board, an international coalition to serve approximately 2200 people. A floating palace, and we the prepaid kings and queens for seven days. Grand chandeliers, exotic flower arrangements, excellent art, elegant hallways, endless banks of very good food on the buffets, and a dinner menu equal to high-end restaurants. Or you could choose one of the several specialty restaurants.

For entertainment—forgive me for the complete tour but we're virgins, after all—after the Vegas-type main stage show in the evenings, you can ramble to B. B. King's Blues Club, or to the singing and piano-playing duo called Billboard Onboard. Or there's Lincoln Center Stage, a string and piano quintet from Ukraine, licensed by the Lincoln Center.

All this of course against a backdrop. The 180-degree turn from the one that glitters, that smiles. It's been a hard year for us. Hard several years. Let's say five, to be exact. Politically, we've watched the slow-motion demolition of what we've seen as the best of our country's ideas, attitudes. Meantime, there was my cancer, Jerry's three surgeries, two on his back, one hip replacement. You should see his back, all achingly twisted. He can walk only short distances.

However, on a cruise, you can go places while sitting in a deck chair. This is what we were thinking. The ports show up, one after the other. It's like you're watching a movie of the world. Even if you go ashore, each port is itself a movie, directed and choreographed for you to have an "experience." To see what you desire. To live inside its lineaments.

> *What is it men in women do require?*
> *The lineaments of Gratified Desire*
> *What is it Women do in men require?*
> *The lineaments of Gratified Desire.*

William Blake didn't say "gratified desire." He said "lineaments," only the distinctive features of it. The outline, you might say, of what it might look like if our desires were fulfilled.

We rented a wheelchair for the ship. It's not the first time we've used one, but there is more of a commitment to the chair this time. We thought he'd be better, but the hip and back pain haven't gone away. Walking's possible, but only for short distances, slowly. So, there will be a whole week to wheel him around. The 180 doesn't leave us, even here.

There's an art to pushing. I can tell you now: don't follow behind anyone too closely; watch the feet; don't crash them into a doorway or anyone else; back into elevators; lift the front wheels a bit at the metal seams in the hallways; watch for bumps; warn the person in the chair before you go speeding to make it over one; better yet, take the smoothest route; back down inclines if you can.

We get Jerry out of the chair, fold it skinny, and then get him back in, to make it around crowded furniture. It fits in our stateroom only when folded, so we have to maneuver ourselves inside, holding the heavy door (everything on a ship is weighted) to push the chair in and against the wall. Little tricks.

Life has been wheelchairs for a while. My father, over in Willow Cottage near us, having only one leg, is "confined" as they say, to a wheelchair. I am, of late, a pusher of people, a follower-behind in the ever-shifting exhibition life presents now, a consumer of sights, of waves and sunsets, of decorative desserts. I push Jerry through the ground floor of Harry Truman's Little White House, the same in Hemingway's Key West house with its thirteen cats.

I am tired. In general. And awkward in this new world. There have been the surgeries, the pain, the surgeries. It all costs. It costs a forward momentum, it stalls. It stops the mind so there is the staring out at the sea. It separates one from the pack. Or, rather, it situates one between worlds.

Who is the pack? I thought I was a part of one, but this year's politics have demonstrated to me that my country is replete with people I don't understand at all. And, too, I can add my poor hearing to the lack of understanding. Conversations go on around me and I miss approximately one-sixth of what's said. Speech is like a paper snowflake: many holes, but I can pretty much discern the shape by what's left.

Confusion is scary, of course. It draws us inward. Makes us fierce nationalists, racists, homophobes. Even hearing loss. It gets hard to keep trying to be in the conversation, it's easier to back away, stare at a painting. Read a book.

What isolates us on the vast sea and what saves us are often the same thing. Books have saved me this year. I've brought my Kindle onboard and also a hard-copy book in case the sun's too bright for the screen. Back in the fall I read all of the Maisie Dobbs series of mystery novels, by Jacqueline Winspear, and then moved on to Louise Penny's excellent series of Inspector Gamache mysteries. One after the other, sometimes out of order, but then the narrative correcting itself in the next, as I discover the why of it. I should say, this is all totally uncharacteristic of the old me. At the last page, barely a breath between, I click to the next book in the series. $9.99 after $9.99, oblivious to my loyalty to local bookstores, oblivious to the other, headier, books piled on my future-reads shelf.

Actually, in a way, I congratulate myself. I'm reading what I once considered junk. I'm allowing myself to wallow in books that aren't remotely "useful." I'm living in the moment, taking in the clues, excited to find the killer. At the moment things look hopeless, terrible, but, finally, all will be well. All manner of things will be well.

In the one I just finished, Gamache's assistant, Jean Guy Beauvoir, has been lured back into a near-fatal addiction to OxyContin. The author describes the feeling when the drug hits the bloodstream—a great warm sigh, an easing, a sense that all's right with the world. "Beauvoir felt the pills take hold. Felt the pain finally recede, the hole heal," she writes.

Back to the ship, the floating miracle-machine where the goal is exactly a warm easing. Ah, cruising. It started in 1844, when the Peninsular and Oriental Steam Navigation Company began carrying passengers, for pure pleasure, from England to Gibraltar, Malta, and Athens. More and more such ships were commissioned in the latter part of the nineteenth century. The fancier, the more takers. As airplanes eroded the practical need, cruise liners devoted themselves to luxury—excursions, guided tours, dancing, multistory atriums, glass elevators, staterooms with balconies outnumbering interior sleeping quarters.

I step out onto our own stateroom balcony, tiny, but big enough for two lounge chairs and a small table. Way below, one after another of the tethering lines are hauled in, starting with the thin-as-thread ones, how they look from up here, fastened to the next in thickness, and so on to the final massive lines, sucked into the ship. Our bags show up. We put away everything in tiny shelves, tiny closets. And then we we're at sea, borne away into the vastness.

The mind rushes to fill the space with ideas. Or with floating images. It's like dreaming—open, and randomly swinging between happy and sad.

A flash in my mind: of night, at our cottage in the woods, miles from much of anything. Jerry's standing, unable to bend or sit, in such pain I call 911. He's only been out of the hospital a few days. The crew that shows up, burly guys from the volunteer fire department first. Then the ambulance crew. Six men in that tiny space, going over their checklist. Comic, until you look at Jerry. So, off he goes to the ER, me following with Wally our cat. Who knows how long this time? Sure enough, it's several days to seemingly resolve the hip pain. Then back to our condo. Then two days later I call our neighbors who own a wheelchair. Please come. Jerry now has a fever and is coughing terribly. Back to the hospital, this time with pneumonia.

Images become glued to the mind when emotions are high, when adrenalin is pumping. Me, in the cottage bedroom, my mind floundering with what to do. Me, in the condo, breakfast ready, watching Jerry bent from coughing, feeling his forehead. Really, the choice is choiceless. The floundering is only that of a ship changing course. Seemingly confused, but it always has been in motion toward what's next.

Me, staring at the Caribbean, these images arriving from the deep. From whence Jonah, Ahab, Captain Cook, Captain Hook, Lord Nelson, Robinson Crusoe, from whence me, once floating in an amniotic sea, my body holding in itself even now the sway of forces, leaning over the highly polished wooden rail, all motion, nothing still. Nothing entirely interior or exterior.

Me, staring: motion is our native land. We are forever at sea. Nonetheless, we are forever tied to the mast, tying ourselves to the mast. We want to be happy. Here are the ingredients: open sea, a cadre of servants, breakfast in bed, music. We want to be happy. We draw a boundary around happy and set unhappy outside it. We pull up the drawbridge. When unhappy gets in, when someone falls ill on the ship, there is a call to donate blood, and when that doesn't suffice, the patient is taken away by helicopter. Rid of the trouble, we go on. We are going nowhere that matters, only to more shores, more beaches, more sunshine. We are invited to participate in a 5K walk around the promenade deck, for cancer research. The sunshine of our benevolence makes us smile.

Not to sneer. Not at all. We are neither the heroes nor the villains of whatever reverie shows up while we lean over the railing. We are the necessary components, the passengers. We go ashore at Grand Turk and, in spite of sunscreen, hat, and umbrella, Jerry gets a terrible sunburn. A sunburn was called for, I guess, to demonstrate that we'd come to the land of the sun, and Jerry was the one to get it.

What the sea sings: Are you tired of your litany of troubles? Do you think you have suffered? I am uninterested in the suffering that happens within me; I love all of my ingredients. Do you think you've dealt with things well, or that you've accomplished nothing? I have no idea what you're talking about.

The Holland America line owns its own island, Half Moon Cay, in the Bahamas. Jerry stays onboard with his sunburn, I board the tender, the boat that ferries us to shore. *Tender*, in its multitude of meanings, has this one, too. But I hear *gentle, fragile, vulnerable*. I add them to this ferrying, this attending. I am so strange! I am sure I'm the only one on the boat occupied with etymology.

We are deposited on shore, passed again through a checkpoint and on to a wide circle of shops and excursion kiosks. I've signed up for the ecoexcursion in a glass-bottom boat, but it's not yet time to leave, so I walk down the perfectly groomed beach, past paddleboards, kayaks, and snorkel equipment for rent, past small multicolored wooden cabanas you can also rent, a home away from your home-away-from-home for your family, your group. Shade from the sun you've come here to bask in.

It is a strange feeling, in this constructed place. It reminds me of Vegas, an entirely artificial world that makes me marvel at the ingenuity of humans while at the same time I feel claustrophobic, uneasy. Would walking the alleys of Mumbai be more "real," do you think? I walk along the brick paths just off the beach, looking for the border where the land quits holding its pretty breath and relaxes to its normal slouch. Where the garbage trucks rumble through, emptying the trash cans.

Yet here I am, glad to be warm, loving the sand on my feet, the glistening sea. The list of excursions for the day didn't mention that we could spend the whole time on the beach, so I've come unprepared. I didn't wear my swimsuit and I've forgotten sunscreen. I walk back to the center of the "village" to the first aid station. The helpful woman says they have none for sale, but she squeezes out enough to get me through the morning.

Our small group climbs onto an open-air trolley to be taken to the cove for our excursion, which is pretty interesting, although our guide has such a strong accent, I miss a lot. She says only forty-five people actually live on the island, and they're service workers. She stands at the front of our little boat and shows us examples of the corals she's pointing to through the glass bottom. It all looks colorless down there. I ask if the corals here are still healthy. "Yes!" she replies emphatically, with no other comment. Best not get started on that ecological issue, it seems.

My mind crossing over again: when we lived in Delaware, I could never escape the feeling of never being able to escape. The most isolated woods were fringed with the faint roar of traffic. Or a plaque, or a marked path. When we moved to northern Michigan, I could feel the rambling, rangy edge, the rotten fence, the truck with rusted fenders, the potholes, the fertile holes in civilization.

I did not yet know I had cancer when Jerry and I took our first trip to Michigan's Upper Peninsula. There was a freedom of mind, then. We reached the tip of Grand Marais and stared out into Lake Superior. Why did I feel so electric? I told Jerry at the time I knew how the pioneers felt, how Louis and Clark felt, Balboa, and the rest. Not an epiphany, but a lightness, a wild surmise. The virgin mind, exuberant with endless possibilities, no clue as to what's next.

Holland America Line bought Little San Salvador, this 2400-acre island, from its previous owners for $6 million, spent $15 million to spruce it up, and renamed it Half Moon Cay. Cruise Critic says it looks like "a movie set of a beach. The sand is pristinely white, with nary a scratchy shell or untoward piece of seaweed. The sea is warm, but not too warm, and turquoise, just like all the postcards."

Desire is perpetual, right? It's an idea, a brochure of a cruise ship where all prayers have been answered, cancers cured, backs straightened, pain gone. Desire is always out there, not here. Even when we set foot on board, the heavy luggage of our desire comes with us. I'm thinking, then, desire must be an ingredient of reality. An energy like the molecules we're made of.

We are at sea. We are unable to come to shore in the Dominican Republic because the water is too rough. We are at sea another day. We lose track. I get a very expensive hot-rocks massage from a pretty young Swedish woman I can barely understand. I do understand her to say that my skin is very dry, and I should buy her special brush to get rid of dead cells. I should brush in the direction of my lymph nodes. And I should buy some of her herbal scented oil.

And then we disembark. The word makes me think of a tree, undressing. Leaving the part of itself behind that's been making itself presentable to the world. What's left is tender, raw. We collect our suitcases packed with dirty laundry. A ship's helper wheels Jerry to the port building, and he manages to climb the three stairs onto the bus. Carefully. One, then one, then one more.

Survival

Imperceptibly, the white pine has grown so tall no one can see what's happening up there. Dirt has mounded at its base, the underside asserting itself: a bulge of the invisible. You can see the tree from far down the lake. It was planted ninety years ago by my father and his brother. They put a fresh gar under it, prehistoric nourishment. The gar's needle-nose is full of sharp teeth, likely floating loose under there, still.

The gar is under the worry. We have envisioned trees falling on the old cottage, especially this tree, yet it has stood through Warren Harding's quick, electric ascension and short term before his death, after which the scandals besmirched his name, followed by silent Cal, his wry wit and small government policies, followed by Hoover, Mr. Efficiency, who couldn't fix the Great Depression's downward spiral, followed by FDR's New Deal and Truman's Marshall Plan, followed by General Eisenhower, and then. . . .

. . . I was beginning to remember for myself. There was beginning to be me. There was beginning to be Kennedy, Johnson, Nixon, Ford, Carter, Reagan, Bush, Clinton, Bush, and miraculously, Obama, and then what happened next.

Come gar, from your one-hundred-million-year past. Drift motionless near the surface waiting for smaller fish to swim by. Keep on living even in extremely inhospitable waters. Fill your swim bladder with air to supplement your gills. Breathe in, breathe out. I like to hear of survival.

Hold on, pine tree, for your hundred years, maybe two hundred. Wait out the thunderstorms. No, waiting is a kind of longing, so I must instead ask for for repetitive needling, shedding, I must ask for cones, which contain the longing but don't themselves long. The longing is bigger, and swallows its own tail, so to speak.

Sunrise comes to the top of the pine long before it reaches the ground. Beyond the tree is the lake, and across the lake, sunset and after-glow. The tree is so close to the water it must have some lake under it. Maybe the gar is swimming in the saturated sandy soil.

And in the remains of the years of forest, of logging, of regrowth. The dead gar's molecules, the sky's investment of air, woven in by the worms. Zebra mussels thrown to shore to die, and here come the dab-bling mallards, a brood depleted, no doubt, by the giant snapping turtle that lumbers along underwater near the dock. The turtle's head and neck rise like a fist from the surface. It needs all its muscle, since it can't retract into its shell. Come snapper, come mallards, duke it out above the confusing invisible currents.

The tree has grown too straight to shadow the water. It is the kind perfect for ships' lumber, a prize in the old days, why the Michigan forests were clear-cut. The Iroquois, Ojibwa, Zhingwaak, called it the Tree of Peace. When I refer to it as *It*, I have already left the Peace and have collected my little army of words, as if I could add a layer of bark, for protection.

My death slowly begins to feel warm and familiar, my tiny use of oxygen, my swimming waves that forget themselves immediately. I have learned to sleep on my back. I have come to prefer it, lying there as if dead already, like a felled tree, or one that has grown tired and come to prefer softening into the earth. Into its smell, made of itself.

I am a little comforted by the thought of leaving the pine behind, alive; maybe it will see the New World. The United States has been putting itself together all these years with the fuss and bother, the frantic losses, the space races, the brutal wars. And the guiding power of the sun, of gravity, each balanced and giving enough to allow for incursions.

It is all sad, I must say, only if you want to have love in the form you're used to, have the voices you're used to, the sand and waves you've grown up with. If you're willing to see what's next, it may not be so bad, but you won't know, since you're not available to say. The word "bad" was your word. The pine tree has never heard of it.

Techie Audiology

Desmond Bates, the hard-of-hearing sixty-something hero of *Deaf Sentence*, by David Lodge, goes to a loud party and ends up as director of a thesis about suicide by a deeply disturbed grad student because he can't hear what she's asking him. The novel is full of hilarious misunderstandings, like "Crap and Sargasso" for "Braque and Picasso." But it comes down to this, as Lodge writes: "Deafness is a kind of pre-death, a drawn-out introduction to the long silence into which we will all eventually lapse."

I was maybe thirty when tinnitus began to sing its one relentless, disembodied note in me. I can't remember if I suspected hearing loss, but I doubt it, because when some of the circles on the graph fell below the "normal" line, I remember being truly shocked. The first small hint of incipient old age. Me: "What if it gets worse?" Audiologist: "You'll get hearing aids." Oh, lord, I thought. Me: "What if it gets even worse?" Audiologist: "You'll learn sign language."

Nice to have options. But that's the truth of it. You can't get it back. When I was teaching at the university, my hearing gradually got so much worse that I would have to ask students to repeat way too many times. Embarrassing. And you can't carry on a decent classroom discussion. I would sometimes ask students to paraphrase what the previous one said. I am nothing if not inventive. Once when I was assigned a classroom with poor acoustics, after the first couple of days, I made up some excuse to ask for a different room. Since all the good ones were gone, we ended up in a basement dungeon. I must have given the students some reason. But they endured. And, frankly, the decor of the room was not of much interest to them.

I'll bet they saw the problem. But no one said a thing. I could see them sometimes look at each other when I'd ask a student to repeat more than once. That kind of blankness that says, "Oh, yes, we're not going to give a sign we see what's going on."

Q: Why don't—why didn't—I just announce that I couldn't hear? A: Because people will really try to speak up, for maybe three minutes, after which they return to their set point. And some people's "speaking up" isn't enough. Especially students. Some people swallow their words, or mumble. Some people can't articulate to save their souls.

First, I was prescribed only one hearing aid. For the ear that was the worst. As the audiologists say, the ear that "showed the most change." I first wore it to dinner with a couple we really didn't want to be with anyway. Maybe with people we enjoyed and trusted, I might have told them how strange things sounded, and why. It was like hearing through a barrel. Your brain has to get used to it. After a while, it seems normal. "Normal" changes. And of course I was embarrassed. In my mind it was like hiding a mouthful of false teeth.

That hearing aid was a little flesh-colored thing molded to fit inside my ear entirely. You could see it, so I made sure to wear my hair so that it fell over my ear. Unless my hairdresser cut it too short, in which case I yanked on it trying to make it grow faster. Hearing aids then were analog. They had a small range of possibilities and could be adjusted only in the audiologist's office. Because the speaker and receiver were right next to each other within the same tiny chunk of plastic, they were prone to a lot of feedback.

As my hearing "changed" more, I began to realize that I was exhausted after every conversation involving more than one or two people. The last few years of teaching in my low-residency MFA program, I would come home after the ten intense days utterly, unnaturally drained. It is a terrible struggle to stay tuned with every fiber of your being to the next word. Fiber, literally: every one of the poor, damaged cilia you have left in your ears. After a while, the balance tips, and it gets not worth it.

You walk into a conversation. Six or eight people. Things get interesting. Someone says something funny. Everyone laughs. You don't know what's funny. Do you stop the whole thing dead in its tracks to say, "What? I didn't catch the joke." What's worse than a retold joke? Not much. Or, at any point, if you say, "I didn't get what you said," the momentum is shot, everyone feels guilty and tries to include you, but, well, the momentum is shot. It's not a matter of being brave enough to let people know what you need. It's a matter of boring even yourself with the intrusions. Better just try to appear to keep up.

Coping mechanism: become expert at guessing. You're at a loud party. You catch one word of a conversation. You think it's "kayak." You're pretty sure the conversation is about a recent kayak trip. You wait a bit and you say, "I had a great kayak trip through the Chain of Lakes last summer." But what if you misheard? What if she'd said "wildcat?" Even if you got it right, you begin to suspect you sound narcissistic because you're not responding to her actual story.

However, life has much improved in the semisilent world! I now have amazing digital hearing aids that cost as much as a used car. You wouldn't know I was wearing them. Tiny and as powerful as a long-distance FM station. I put them in as soon as I get up and the world goes from silent to full of tics and bumps and rattles and crow calls, the steady background that saves people from being alone. The receivers pick up sounds from all directions, so it's pretty close to "real" hearing. The little buggers are working their heads off inside themselves, sending and receiving signals that speak to each other, assessing the quality of sound in the room, adjusting as they can. And, my phone can send the speaker's voice directly into my hearing aids. Also, I have a little box by the TV, so that all I have to do is reach up and click at my right ear to get the TV sound directly into my ears. All that plus closed captioning almost saves me.

When my father became almost deaf, I had my old hearing aids reset for him. He wore them until he died. They were digital, pretty good, but vastly inferior to the next ones, which my husband is wearing at present. They're not Bluetooth-enabled, he can't use them with his iPhone, or with a TV box, but the sound is subtle and high-quality. I save the best ones for myself. The greatest good to the one with the greatest need.

The audiologist's array is a technological wonderland. On her screen are two separate graphs, each ear's successes and failures. You can see the dotted line that represents normal hearing. You can see the shaded area between what the hearing aids can do and what would be ideal. You can determine the frequencies that are comfortable for you. You can have infinite adjustments in pitch, tone, and feedback reduction. All this does almost save you.

Almost. Does no good to kick a dead horse. Last week there were a group of us sitting in the living room talking, and I suddenly thought, no, this won't do. I'm picking up only about 80 percent of the conversation. You'd think, well, that's not so bad. But try slicing 20 percent off the tops of letters in a sentence. See how much you recognize.

Coping mechanism: someone tells a joke, everyone laughs. I have gotten really good at laughing at the right time and the right level to indicate I'm in on it but not to implicate me in fully understanding, in case there's a test.

So, this week I went back to my techie audiologist, who added a second program to my hearing aids. Number one is the broad-angle hearing that most approximates normal life. Number two is the narrowed focus that points my receivers directly ahead of me, softening down all ambient sound. Think of it as the difference between sunlight shining everywhere and a searchlight. Sometimes you need a searchlight.

There's a newer model out. It speeds up the internal processing, so you hear the sounds closer to having them arrive unimpeded by a transmitter and receiver. If I need to, I'll jump to those. Essentially, you might say, I'll buy a new car when my old one is only two-and-a-half years old.

Processing is really the whole ball game. As my hearing has "deteriorated" (another audiologist no-no word), I have much more trouble keeping up with speech. It goes too fast. The body is desperately trying to read all the signals—facial, body, tone, context—to translate into meaning. It takes valuable time to move through that sequence. Meantime, the conversation has moved on. Oh, rats, what were they saying?

The last-ditch remedy, at least for now, is a cochlear implant. It's very different from a hearing aid. Hearing aids amplify sounds. A cochlear implant is an incredibly complicated system that bypasses the ear and heads directly to the auditory nerve, which sends the signals to the brain. The brain figures out that the signals are sound. It's not the same as "hearing," but it does allow many nearly deaf people a decent simulation of it.

I got my father a phone with a screen that prints the words out as the person on the other end is talking. Miraculous. We had it installed at his assisted living place just in time for him to have a real conversation with his Texas daughter, my sister, before he died. His isolation was almost unbearable. This helped a bit.

Everything connects. Even the trees have their social network. I have been reading about isolation. Social isolation and loneliness are not the same thing, says the National Institute for Health.[*] 28 percent of older people live alone, but that doesn't mean they're all lonely. They may have a great network of friends and family.

Losing a sense of connection and community changes a person's perception of the world. Chronic loneliness makes us feels threatened and mistrustful, which activates a biological defense mechanism, writes Steve Cole, director of the Social Genomics Core Laboratory at the University of California, Los Angeles.[†] "Loneliness acts as a fertilizer for other diseases," he writes. "The biology of loneliness can accelerate the buildup of plaque in arteries, help cancer cells grow and spread, and promote inflammation in the brain leading to Alzheimer's

[*] "Social Isolation, Loneliness in Older People Pose Health Risks," *NIH: National Institute on Aging Newsletter*, April 23, 2019, n.p.

[†] Brent Edwards, "The Future of Hearing Aid Technology," *PMC Journal* (March 2007): 31–45.

disease." Besides Alzheimer's, you have a higher risk for high blood pressure, heart disease, obesity, a weakened immune system, anxiety, depression, cognitive decline, and death.

We need our mutually supportive web, people talking to each other, hugging, visiting. If you're ripped out of the web, or if a disability like hearing loss yanks you out of it, you lose many of your nutrients. You wither. We need to hear and be heard. How toxic it would be, I think, to have a spouse who doesn't listen to you, or to grow up unheard or even unspoken to in a meaningful way!

Then there's shame. Humans are programmed to prefer wholeness, symmetry. To react against difference. So, considering our great need to accept diversity, teachers have been emphasizing inclusion. Teaching that it's not okay to exclude the atypical, the kid with a limp, the old man with a cane. People instinctively smile and open doors for my husband, with his bent back and his cane. Kids on the playground—the well-taught ones—will reach out to the kid with the limp, out of a learned sense of social responsibility. Not because they desire the presence of that kid, who will inevitably slow down the game. But the less well-taught children will tease and bully.

When we're at the movies, or at the symphony, I look down the rows in front of me and see the little gleaming curves behind the ears, otherworldly accoutrements. A lot of retired people live in our semi–resort community. For years, men have been reluctant to wear hearing aids because they're visible, and a symbol of aging, of shameful loss of masculine power. But now we know the damaging effect of social isolation. So they wear them. Women, of course, hide them behind their hair.

Hide, because shame is primal. To be different, to stand out feels like shame. You've failed to measure up to some ideal state, which in this culture is youth. Shame on you. It falls on you like molten lava. It is all over you. I forgot to say, audiologists don't call them hearing "aids"; they're hearing "instruments." You're supposed to see a hip young man with one of those wireless phones draped over his ear. Not your great-uncle's clumsy chunks of flesh-colored plastic.

Shame is primal. There was my seriously brain-damaged brother at home, who had frightening seizures, who could hardly speak and would sometimes cry out instead of speaking, who lurch-walked, when he could walk. There was my family, a capsule of isolation. Isolated from lunches and dinners with friends, parties—my mother, sweet as she was, socially awkward and afraid, my father, somewhere on the autism spectrum, behaving not at all "normally." It all felt shameful to me. My house was four walls of shame to be hidden away from the outside world.

I was a capsule of misery, of difference. I carried it out the door with me. Every teenager feels her difference, but mine felt more awful. Okay, I suspect if a group of teenagers were together in a therapy group, you'd likely see that each one feels the most awful! The point is, we each held our individual shame. If we'd known how to share it, it would have hurt less.

I'm thinking that memoirs, though, often parade separateness, shame, in a kind of reverse egotism. They say, "Look at how awful things were for me, how isolated, how deprived, how I survived." The survival has a lot to do with the words on paper. And if you can't hear, words on paper will save you. They will organize your loneliness, invite someone to read it.

Bluetooth is coming closer and closer to saving you. I mean me. My cell phone, which has its own Bluetooth, transmits directly to my hearing aid.

A heck of a lot is demanded of a hearing aid. Think of what your natural ears are supposed to do. Pick up sounds from all over, signal the exact pitch and tone that allows you to tell what direction it's coming from and how far away it is. Your ears talk to each other through your brain. The more subtle the digital processing gets, the closer all that can be mimicked in hearing aids.

Noise reduction has been improved so much that the hearing aids notice feedback almost immediately and change signals to stop it from happening. My mother's hearing aids squealed if you got anywhere close to her ears. My earlier ones did, too. I learned to hug carefully, turn my head just right. My new ones hardly make a sound.

I once said if I had to choose, I'd rather losing hearing than sight. "Because sight is so obvious," I wrote, "its loss so easy to feel." I have completely changed my mind. Hearing is a much more direct path to each other. I could sit in a room, blind, and have rich, meaningful conversations. I would not be isolated, even if the gorgeous moon out the window is lost to me, the expanse of the bay. Even the expression on my husband's face would be lost. But there would be his voice, which happens to be rich and resonant. I've told him I married him for his voice. It carries so much warmth and self-awareness.

Grass-Covered Chest

All we perceive at any instant is a slice of
the whole. Our sense of time: an illusion.
Nothing passes; nothing changes.

—Hermann Minkowski,
Einstein's teacher

The small chest used to be covered with a woven grass fabric, but by the time we got it, the cover was tattered beyond repair. We tore it off, and even after the sanding, the grassy marks were still there, making a subtle design, a stubble design. There are small, squat legs and a hinge. Inside is where we keep some of the puzzles. The chest was Grandmother Brown's. I can almost see it in the old days, but not quite. I'm not sure where to place it in her house. I know where the piano was, in the dining room with the glittering beveled glass windows. I think it was beside that, but it's too small for what I have in mind, with my brother's record player on it. He loved that record player. He would lean over it, drooling, and try to sing along. He had some words by then.

I remember my mother carrying him as an infant up the stairs and through the door of our house on Garth Avenue. I don't remember this. I have to have some place to start, in my head: the little chest that morphs into what must have been a larger one, and then before that, in some sort of sequence, a baby. Virginia Woolf called memory a seamstress, "and a capricious one at that." ("Memory runs her needle in and out, up and down, hither and thither. We know not what comes next, or what follows after.")

I remember a small being, in blankets. Maybe Mark, maybe earlier, maybe my sister. Memory often doesn't know what to do with its own images. This was before any sense of trouble. I remember hearing "diarrhea," and what Dr. Dexheimer, the family physician, was doing, unsuccessfully, to stop it. I remember chatter and tension the way a child does, not comprehending much, but feeling. I was seven. Then the hush, the dissatisfaction with the doctor, the talk of what to do, or was that later? Of Mark's odd, convulsive movements. Or was that later? I remember staying with my other grandparents, Mother's parents, who lived next door, while Mother took him to St. Louis to the children's hospital. My father heading out on his brother's motor scooter for St. Louis, 125 miles on that tiny thing. My grandparents' controlled anger, their urging him to drive, to take their car, use their gas. This is how he was. Terrified of spending. I remember these things as large, upper forces, moving a bit like seagrass, pulling me this way and that.

Memory is not a thing, of course. It's more like a superpower. It's Mnemosyne, the ancient Greek Titan, goddess of memory and remembrance and the inventor of language and words. How desperately she was needed before there was writing! How deftly the writing pulls at the threads, the web-like pattern of cells scattered throughout the brain that combine and reassemble impressions. The convergence of sight, smell, taste, touch, hearing, and thinking create what seemed to be real, what seems to be real. I think of "convergence" and just now Thomas Hardy's poem "The Convergence of the Twain" comes to me, about the sinking of the Titanic when it hit an iceberg: "The Spinner of the Years / Said, 'Now!' And each one hears / And consummation comes, and jars two hemispheres."

My brain catches the word "convergence" and sees all that: Hardy's poem on the page, each stanza shaped like a small ocean liner, the conjured image from long ago when I first read it, combined with Leonardo DiCaprio and Kate Winslet standing at the prow, falling in love, you know they are, you know that. Like the ship, this image is the "sign that they were bent / On paths coincident / On being anon twin halves of one august event." You know the poem. I know the poem, that is.

I know the chest. I knew it when it was whole. Maybe it had toys in it, a little red tinplate boat with a propeller that turned. I collect the few images left.

What must it have been like, to be my mother, alone with Mark at the hospital? I have not seen her well enough. I have thought of her as weak, but now, at my age, I change my mind. I think she was pliable, which is not the same thing. She must have stood over him there, afraid and sad. Already she was unhappy with her marriage, but she knew what she had to do: first this, and then that, because this is what life required of her. Her parents despised my father with the patient silence of devout Christians who are not supposed to think bad thoughts. But this was 1951. They would have never been complicit in their daughter's divorce. She knew she was in for this, this marriage, and loved him, I think, with the baffled love that includes a timid rage. Something was missing in him, a blank blip in his emotions, that she kept trying to fill. No one knew anything then about autism.

And Mark was on the verge of dying. But he didn't die. Gradually his diarrhea diminished. Gradually his damaged mind became apparent. You would think I would have been more aware, being old enough. I was running through creek beds, digging holes, catching fireflies and tadpoles. Leave it to them, the adults, their tension, their endless talk, and their silences. Leave it to them to cheer when he could finally scoot himself along in a walker.

Not true. I must have been a fetcher and a wiper, a helper of all sorts. I know because it is in my nature to do that. I am trying to recall as if it matters to recall. Finally, no one will remember, will they? Yet as friends die—they're doing that, lately—I see that memory, even if it only lasts our lifetime, is how we reverence the very act of living, of having lived. My father always said he wanted his body dumped in a garbage can or some such, since it won't matter when he's dead. You could blame that on his autism, but I saw his refusal to accept the reverence as his fear of dying, a strange reversal that can't bear to see how it happens, to imagine it happening.

When my friend Harris died suddenly of a massive heart attack, his friends dredged up as many memories as we could, while scenes from his life flashed on the screen behind us. This was his life. This was a life. Here is the evidence. It mattered.

That was my life, in Columbia, Missouri, in those first years after my brother was born. Inside my mind and my body somewhere must be the emotional residuals. I hung out with my friend Sharon, whose father managed the cemetery next to our school. We climbed on tombstones and tried to pry open crypts. I spent the night at her house, and we stole candy from a store across Broadway. We climbed out her window in early morning, took our candy, and walked down to watch the Wabash come in at the station.

Now I recall the tension around my friendship with her. Nana tried to say she wasn't the kind of person I should be friends with; my father said it was none of her business; my mother was, as always, stretched between, trying to say what her mother wanted her to say without making my father mad. Nana was right. Sharon was harbinger of my attraction to rawness. I was made to visit Julie Glenn's new house in the suburbs. Her father owned the prominent shoe store downtown. I was made to visit Prella Phillips's house on the curving road in front of the park. Her father was an eminent professor. In her back yard was the most elaborate dollhouse I had ever seen, big enough to walk into. Her yard was full of flowers and carefully cut grass. We were served cookies on a tray. I think I felt vaguely sick: with jealousy, with inferiority, with a kind of boredom. I can't say now.

Memory moves uncontrollably in all directions: in this case, spurred on by the little chest. And here comes the rawness, up from under. My life felt raw. My father seemed like a caged animal. Fierce, raging, and electrically attractive. My brother threw himself forward, unannounced, in radical seizures. He cut himself, he bled. My mother cried. There was the radio and there was singing and unpredictable excitement. My father carved a huge propeller for his bike and drove it around town until he was told it was unsafe, with no guard. So he rode it out in the country. He blew up condoms in the basement for us to play with as balloons. I had no idea what they were originally intended for, but the air was clearly charged around them. I wanted to show Nana. Did I? My mother scolded him. This only one of the times I was privy to information I was too young to understand, only to feel the naughtiness, the enticement. They made perfectly good balloons, he said, with his little-boy mischief-maker smile.

Sharon's life was raw enough. Her father dug graves. On the other edge of the cemetery Black people lived. Or were they poor whites? We would walk that way sometimes, where large women sat on porches and children played barefoot in the dirt road. I may be dramatizing this. I have inherited drama. I have created scenes.

Mark grew. We all took care of him the best we could. He learned to walk; he learned to say enough words to communicate; he got a bad case of the flu and gradually declined to permanent invalidism, lying in bed, having his diapers changed. The last two years of his life he lived in an institution. He died at twenty-four. The facts, of course, are only pinpoints on a map. They leave out everything that matters.

By this time, I had two children of my own and was just beginning my second marriage, the one that cured me of any desire for drama. My memory of this marriage lives in my bones and muscles, too raw for language, really. I've tried, and then erased what I've written. I married a tsunami and spent twelve years exhausted with the effort to hold down the flying debris and keep my children as safe as possible. I should say, I did not know what safe was, then, having little experience with it.

In Dante Gabriel Rossetti's painting of Mnemosyne, also titled *Lamp of Memory and Ricordanza*, she is holding up a small chalice, apparently to fill the lamp she holds in the other hand. She is very still, sedate, with heavy Pre-Raphaelite hair and green draped gown. Her almost somnolent eyes appear not to be recollecting, but the way it looks to me, suffering, enduring. Her lamp itself is made of what appears to be flames on all sides. Rossetti has Inscribed on the frame of the painting, "Thou fill'st from the winged chalice of the soul / Thy lamp, O Memory, fire-winged to its goal." What is the goal, then, of memory, that it is so full of fire to get there? What is the goal when there is suffering in the memories?

I once thought I could re-remember and fix things retroactively. I thought I could contain and arrange by writing. But there is Memory, held valiantly in its chalice, only to pour itself out, unbidden, to flame the pot.

Here is a memory that should have been warning enough of the tsunami: my next-door neighbor offered to get me one of those cone-shaped fireplaces for my den, for cheap. I said sure. It was delivered and I had trouble getting it installed properly, so I called the store. Sears called back to say they had no record of selling us the fireplace and would like to send a team of people out to uncover the circumstances (turns out my neighbor was basically a mobster). My new husband—an articulate PhD candidate—took the call. He launched into a story about how I couldn't come to the phone, and that we were a Christian family (strong southern accent added at this point, plus appropriate clichés) and that he was offended at their implications. He grew loud and animated. He would not let me talk to them. I had no say in this matter. Truth had no say in the matter. A person could play this way with truth, make up anything, for the heck of it.

The way it feels to me now, my children and I entered an alternate reality. At any moment, the ground could shift. We learned to tiptoe. We learned that to argue was to be engulfed in a barrage of words and just enough of a taste of violence to guess that more could emerge. Why didn't I leave? There was this: some moments of joy, of laughter, and excitement of the good kind, of adventure. And I was stuck. I had quit teaching high school and was studying for my PhD. We had moved to Delaware. I would have to find another job, somewhere, move the kids and me away. Away from their schools, their friends. Did I make a terrible mistake? For that matter, did my mother make a mistake? Is "mistake" a word that has any meaning? There is one thing, then another. We do the best we can with what we have. To imagine a different life is to imagine a different person.

Ah, this started out with a small chest that belonged to my father's mother. I don't know what she used it for, or where she got it. I don't know where it belonged in the house. It simply stands for her, for what I think was her. What I knew of her was mostly her house, its creaky wood floors, its two fireplaces, one in the bedroom, its one bathroom upstairs with claw-foot tub—give me enough time and I'll take you all over the house, from the high sun porch with the box of lead soldiers to the coal chute in the basement and the room full of coal. Somewhere in that house was this small grass-covered chest. I can put it anywhere I want. I can make it stand for a certain chosen beauty. She chose this. Or, she was given it. Or, she brought it with her from her family home. The more I consider the options, the more the chest itself seems like a figment of my imagination, a token of what home means, and beauty.

We have put it in front of the daybeds-turned-couches in the cottage in Michigan. It was refinished by my husband of twenty-seven years. The two of us tend not to invent drama, but drama has of course come to us in all sorts of forms—illness, surgeries, our children's troubles, and the troubles of the world.

Which is to say, life is trouble. *And then you die*, is what's supposed to follow. As if death is the final insult to the string of previous ones. As if. Among the senses, the firing neurons, the patterns of brain activity, can any conclusions be reached? I don't know. "Time is a river that sweeps me along, but I am the river," says Jorge Luis Borges. "It is a tiger that mangles me, but I am the tiger; it is a fire that consumes me, but I am the fire."

I don't know if there's a need for a goal, other than to be completely aware of this gorgeous, extravagant combination of immediacy and memory I'm made of. Memory is ragged, and distorted, kind of like the grass on that chest, only an impression left in the varnish. I am very fond of that little chest. It has small brass handles, I forgot to say. You can easily pick it up, move it around. You could turn it so it opens toward you or away. You could put it anywhere.

Becoming Mrs. Ramsay

My phone says it's 1 degree outside, and minus 2 at the cottages an hour north of here. The snow must be waist-high there, the lake frozen solid and dotted with icehouses, for fishing. The little town of Central Lake will be scraping through another winter, Bachmann's General Store ("If We Don't Have It, You Don't Need It") selling a few dish towels and heating pads until summer, when the children will stand before the wide wooden tray of candy that used to cost a penny each, to choose the number of pieces their parents allow, and, while they're at it, bargain for a bag of plastic insects, or dinosaurs. Adults will buy another iteration of the Central Lake logo sweatshirt or hat.

I used to fear that Central Lake, grown by logging and shrinking by lack of it, would die entirely, but it hangs on, Bachmann's store still in the family, run by Mike Bachmann's niece after he retired, and before that by his father. And the Village Market, formerly Central Foods, is now stocking enough variety to make it possible to mostly shop there instead of driving to Bellaire. There are two car repair shops, a nice library, Madam's Adam's boutique, and the large Blue Pelican restaurant that used to be the Lamplight Inn. There are still several rooms to rent upstairs. My nephew Kevin rented one for himself, his wife, and his son Benjamin when the cottage was too full. He went downstairs at night to ask a question and discovered that the place was entirely dark, no one in the whole building except them. He was so unnerved that the three of them slept huddled in the same bed for the rest of the night.

We've been planning to drive up and paint a few swatches of color on the wall of the little cottage, to choose one, but it's too cold. The polar vortex has held us most of the winter, submerged in cold and snow, our own north pole.

I want to get to this paint job. I'm always eager to do anything that involves the cottages. I should say, last year was the first time I realized I was Virginia Woolf's Mrs. Ramsay. I was picking up fallen branches around the old cottage, painting the green edge of the porch trim to save it one more year from rot, and I thought, yes, I have become the spirit of the place. The comings and goings revolve, now, around me, and when I die, the children and grandchildren will stand on the end of the dock, looking toward town, then south, to the wide part of the lake. Not looking for anything, but recalibrating.

I am standing at the corner of the porch, no, just off the porch to the north side. The cedars that have since been cut down when they threatened the porch are still there, their trunks still thin. My angle of vision is low, because I am nine years old. Old Zip Pixler, as she was called, is standing so that she's between the shining lake and me. She is still wearing her apron. She has walked down their steep hill to say that nothing will be the same, with Brownie gone. My grandmother. My grandmother, my father's mother who has come to my eyes now in place of Zip Pixler, long hair caught up but coming loose and blowing even though she had it bobbed years before she died. She is standing on the little bit of broken sidewalk between the cottage and the lake, looking out, as she did, watching for my father, who has sailed so far out of sight he won't be back in time for supper. Woolf would have put a lighthouse out there, something visible to yearn toward instead of the blank lake after the sailboat has rounded the point.

I had better talk about my grandmother before she fades entirely. She was not beautiful. She had an English receding chin like Eleanor Roosevelt, but she was not unbeautiful. She was tall and slim. She bent to wash or pick up the dish towel with a self-possession, a grace. I can almost hear her voice, but it has mingled with the others now. She had only a high school education, but she took her husband's economics classes, read his books and many others, and, in the way of her generation, taught herself with no thought for degrees. There is a photo of her and my grandfather after some lecture he's given. She's stylishly dressed, brooch at her lapel, confident, for all the world his equal.

In the distortion of angle, memory coming both from my young self and what I set in place of it these years later, objects grow wavy, unsure. The dross of exactness has fallen away and what's left has mingled with the emotion pulled along with it and become a private emblem.

I have become an emblem. I have become all that is imagined about me. Unlike Mrs. Ramsay, I have written and written my life, but I am sure that when the children and grandchildren think of the lake, they put me not at the computer, but walking across on the leaf-path from the little green cottage to the big old cottage, or sitting on the dock in my tan floppy hat, and I am not myself, but symbolic of the lake, of grandmother: the link to various private memories.

There is no one else anymore. Uncle Richmond, who lives down the lake, is forgetting. My father is gone. Someone must step into place or the structure will begin to give way. Small ruptures, and then nothing but banging shutters, mouse droppings. I see Mrs. Ramsay's shawl, wrapped around the boar's skull hung on the wall, because her son James is afraid of its shadow at night. That one emblem of her nurturing, the way the shawl falls loose in the breeze through a window left slightly open for years. That stays with me like my grandmother's black wool swimsuit on the nail in the back bedroom.

What else stays: my father has been out sailing. He comes back and falls to his knees beside the cottage in front of my grandfather. "Oh, father," he cries, "I have sinned and am no longer worthy to be called your son. I have dropped the hammer in the lake." I am standing on the slight rise by the birch, that's no longer there. The rise fits Grandfather perfectly, with his one leg slightly shorter than the other. On this side of the cottage, there is a small flat space, a little stage, a bare spot before the hammock was moved to the nearby cedars. I'm laughing. But there is a reverberation below the surface. My father is afraid of his father. His act is an act, a play on the bible verses he was taught by his grandmother but discarded. But even at my age, I feel the complexity. His father, the successful academic, with all the books, uprightly Victorian. My father, always the misfit, always fiddling with his sailboats in greasy khakis, fired or not rehired from several academic jobs already. How could I not think of the Ramsays? How could this not be my story? Is my father James, the Ramsay son who hates his father, yet who wanted nothing more than his approval, to be noticed? The magnetism of the story is the same.

I wonder about Mrs. Ramsay (who has no first name). She must have carried, like me, the layers. She must have seen ghost trees, ghost people, like the ones I see: great grandparents, grandparents, uncles, aunts, cousins, children, grandchildren. Even the living ones, the children and grandchildren, when they haven't yet arrived for the summer, they're ghosting under the trees that wait for them. I pull the plastic covering off the beds, I dust, I weed whack around the dock. I pass through the ghosts, readying.

This is the summer we will scatter my father's ashes, which at the moment are sitting in a large tin in the back of my closet. His ashes, my aunt Cleone's, and my grandmother's will be, for eternity, in the lake and on the earth around the cottage. Eternity, as they say. "Eternity" the noun that stands for "forever," yet the movement has never stopped. Still, we draw a line. We'll take note. We create a moment when the idea of "cottage" changes generations. When nothing is the same, as we say, meaning, nothing has ever been the same.

Mrs. Ramsay's death happens in one parenthetical note. Sudden. Over. How strange it is. My father had been typing a letter, joking with Judy, his favorite staff person, that morning. He called to ask how I was feeling, after my minor surgery. That evening, one of the aides called me to say he wasn't feeling well. I called him. His breathing sounded awful. He said he'd been in terrible pain all afternoon. He is such a hypochondriac, so I asked, "How are you right this minute?" "Maybe a little better," he said. I told him to ask for a couple of Tylenols and that I'd call the nurse in the morning. But I didn't like the way he sounded: heavy, gasping. Jerry volunteered to check on him. Almost as soon as he walked in the room, my father died.

He was still warm when I got there. Unusually pale, still himself, but he was gone. Who he was had left somehow, some way, through the same mysterious portal that a human enters the world, from the joining of egg and sperm to a kicking, squalling consciousness. Not gone, but departed. Not departed, but a cataclysmic shift. I rubbed his arm, I smoothed his steely gray and still thick hair. I was looking for him, but he had shifted. I was trying to tell him that I loved him, in spite of everything and because of everything, that I remember our lives, all of it, that I had meant to say all that, to say that something had held me back from it, but now, quickly, please, I could say it.

When my friend Tom died. I stood over his still-warm body and made the sign of the cross. What a strange thing for me to do back then, even then, when I was still considering myself an Episcopalian. I needed some bodily expression of my awe, some way to cross the seeming gulf between then and now, between the tangible and intangible. In the parenthesis, Mrs. Ramsay died. What can't be said hovers in brackets. Hovers in what Emerson called the "very high sort of seeing" found in poetry, whatever can't land solidly because it is itself breathing the breath of forms.

The sail breathes the breath of forms. Once you understand the wind on the lake, once you see its pattern of disruption out there, you know to head for it, to let it use you. My father and I are headed back in the sailboat, already way past dinnertime. I am dragging my hand in the water, which refuses to do more than slosh against the side. We are making only a few feet with each tack. I am getting good at finding the slightest movement on the water, the slightest gusts.

Gusts are not the same as wind; wind is not the same as current. Current is what pulls from underneath, north to south, from way up the chain of lakes, fed by small streams, and into the bay, and into Lake Michigan. Current is ponderous, *weight* in Latin. Weighty thoughts, considered thoughts, compared to wind, which drags up waves, whitecaps even. From the south means a storm coming; from the north means clearing skies. Gusts are momentary and mean nothing. Gusts are sudden tears, while the fact of my father's death is ponderous in me.

What has been the play of personalities on what we call "cottage"? Is anything *has been*? Is there ever a time when the resonances die utterly out? The whole second half of *To the Lighthouse* is shaped by the parenthesis. In the photo, I am wearing a sunbonnet, sitting beside my mother, who is dangling her feet in the water. I might start there, but that's arbitrary. So much has happened before. My mother married my father. My father went overseas. And of course before that and before that. And then my mother died, and now my father, and my memory, my imagination have to stand at the hub, with all this twirling around them as if I myself were a maypole.

In a photo, I am at the head of the table on the screened-in porch because it's my seventieth birthday and I have so far survived cancer. My hair is growing in wildly curly and I'm experimenting with color—I look not at all like myself to myself. Everyone is there, Kelly and her family of five, Scott and his family of four, Uncle Dick and Aunt Lee, Jerry. They go around the table to say wonderful things about me. I have survived. I hear their voices but the words are only resonances, their faces dark against the setting sun. Evening is like that there, light slowly sliding under the trees, scooping up the grass, the rocks on shore, the stilled lake. At dinnertime, an intense orange comes at us so that the one at the head of the table, which is me, is unable to see. It is all silhouette. Or, I am unable to see because of my tears.

Virginia Woolf imagined Mrs. Ramsay as the nurturer and matchmaker, whose natural movement was to sweep together the disparate elements of her life. What if she wasn't sweeping together but simply holding the place they set for her? She is at the head of the table because each of the eight children—plus Mr. Ramsay and the artist, the poet, the botanist, the philosopher, and the two other friends—cry out for a head-of-table. For a prow of the boat, an emblem, a way to think about themselves in relation. In relation. People want a cottage, a grandmother, a mother, a father, the comfort of seeing themselves inside of, beside, taking orders from, rebelling against, modeling themselves after.

And then it's gone. Cremation is as strange a thought as death itself, the body forever in parenthesis, no place for the mind to settle. No flowers to place on a grave, no headstone, no chiseled name. The funeral director said if we'd like to see his body one last time, to bring in some suitable clothes and they would have him there for us. "You'll be glad you did," she said. Since he wasn't embalmed, he was of course ice-cold, lying on a disguised ice-cold slab in a small room with space enough only to stand around him. Instinctively, I placed my hands over his, to warm them up. The mind can't move fast enough to encompass the change, to let go of the need to help. The mind can't move fast enough to let go when the body has let go.

"O the mind, mind has mountains, cliffs of fall," I remember Hopkins. I am sitting with my father in his small room at Willow Cottage, trying to keep up with Einstein with him, trying with my bungling, stiff, three-dimensional mind to envision time and space as a fluidity. How is my vision of us now any different from my actually being there? I see us, I am following the drawings he's made on a scrap of typewriter paper. I am following the images in his head. We both have images in our head. Mountains, and cliffs. I try to imagine who he is, he tries to imagine who I am. We are always trying to somehow meet.

When it's warm, in the spring, his daughters will drive to Central Lake, pass Bachmann's store, turn left at the Village Market, cross over the town bridge, and head for the cottage as we have done so many times they are like one time, to say goodbye and to scatter his ashes. If we all have our memories, all different, crisscrossing at points, then who was he? His body, tangible for a hundred years, was always changing. Yet tangible is only an idea based on the distance between observer and observed. To think solid, you have to back off. You have to put together a lot of ideas and images of your own to come up with the person who sits at the head of the table, the "crown jewel," as my nephew David likes to call him. That's David's idea, not mine. There is so much complexity that to assert anything at all is basically a lie. A necessary one, but still.

My nephew Kevin is sure there were ghosts in that long night at the Blue Pelican Inn. I think he's been at the cottage too rarely to have met the ones who live there. I would introduce him, but it doesn't work like that. The ghosts are private, singular. They rise at an intersection that you had to be there for, come into view, and then sink to a transparency. That doesn't mean they aren't there.

Acknowledgments

"Mortality, with Friends," *Los Angeles Review* (2020).

"Grass-Covered Chest," *River Teeth* 20, no. 2 (2019).

"Smoke," *Arts & Letters* (Spring 2019).

"Fingernails, Toenails," *Agni* 88 (2018).

"Survival," *Brevity* 57 (January 2018).

"Donna," *Prairie Schooner* (Summer 2017).

"Inside the Conch Shell," *Georgia Review* (Winter 2016).

"Mirrored Transoms," *River Teeth* 17, no. 2 (2016), reprinted in *Elemental: A Collection of Michigan Creative Nonfiction* (Wayne State University Press, 2018).

"Strong Brown God," *New Letters* 80, no. 2 (2014), first place, *New Letters* essay award.

"Bill's Clay Figures," *Georgia Review* (Fall 2013).

"Your Father, My Father: Volleys," *Great River Review* (Fall/Winter 2012).

"The Moment," *Brevity* 33 (Summer 2010).

"Your Father, My Father: Volleys": Judith Kitchen's entries with permission of Stanley Rubin.

"Pythagorean" by Linda Gregerson quoted with permission.

"Wherever Home Is" by James Wright quoted with permission of Annie Wright.

About the Author

Fleda Brown's tenth collection of poems, *Flying through a Hole in the Storm*, won the Hollis Summers Prize from Ohio University Press. Earlier poems can be found in *The Woods Are On Fire: New and Selected Poems*, chosen for the University of Nebraska Press Ted Kooser Contemporary Poetry series. Her work has appeared three times in *The Best American Poetry* and has won a Pushcart Prize, the Felix Pollak Prize, the Philip Levine Prize, and the Great Lakes Colleges New Writer's Award, and has twice been a finalist for the National Poetry Series. Her memoir, *Driving with Dvořák*, was published by the University of Nebraska Press. She is professor emerita at the University of Delaware and was poet laureate of Delaware from 2001 to 2007.

Praise for *Mortality, with Friends*

"I have long felt that Fleda Brown the poet had an utterly unparalleled capacity to meld keen intellect, extending even to hard science, with exquisite lyrical sensibility. To read these essays, at once heart-rending and reassuring, is to affirm that that capacity applies to her prose as well. It is not mere hyperbole to say that the woman is matchless, whatever her genre."

—Sydney Lea, Vermont poet laureate (2011–2015)

"*Mortality, with Friends* endeavors to gather, to slightly misquote Leonard Cohen's trope, 'gather up the brokenness and bring it to [us] now.' In an age of isolation, Fleda Brown beckons us to draw near and pay heed to the heart's joyous and sorrowful mysteries, the heart's bewilderments, into the maw of which she tenders a 'countervalent language.' This is balm, a splendid feat in essaying: an orderliness, which feels, if not like healing, a sort of palliative against the ineluctable feature of humanity, to wit: we die."

—Thomas Lynch, author of *The Depositions* and *Bone Rosary*

"In Fleda Brown's *Mortality, with Friends*, every life form 'deserves its own kind of honor': the ordinary and extraordinary, the tiny and massive, the political and personal, even an impossibly difficult father residing in that 'deep interior wound we call *parent*.' Like the sailboat of her childhood whose 'sail breathes the breath of forms,' Brown's arresting essays set off to catch the 'pattern of disruption' of memory's ever-changing currents."

—Rebecca McClanahan, author of *In the Key of New York City: A Memoir in Essays*

"Fleda Brown is a writer who cannot look away. In *Mortality, with Friends*, she probes the deep extent of love by way of loss, and in this way honors the hard truths of living. There is sorrow in these pages, but reading I also kept thinking of Dylan Thomas, his line 'Light breaks where no sun shines.'"

—Sven Birkerts, author of *Changing the Subject: Art and Attention in the Internet Age*

"How is it possible to so fiercely and so lovingly hold and shape the truth of a life? I read these essays hungrily, with the attention one pays a trusted guide, and with the deep pleasure one receives from a poet continually stunned into language."

—Lia Purpura, author of *All the Fierce Tethers*